# The New Apprenticeships

Facilitating learning, mentoring, coaching and assessing

POST-16 LEARNING

Most of our titles are also available in a range of electronic formats. To order please go to our website www.criticalpublishing.com or contact our distributor, NBN International, 10 Thornbury Road, Plymouth PL6 7PP, telephone 01752 202301 or email orders@nbninternational.com.

# The New Apprenticeships

## Facilitating learning, mentoring, coaching and assessing

**ANDREW ARMITAGE
AND ALISON COGGER**

POST-16 LEARNING

First published in 2019 by Critical Publishing Ltd





British Library Cataloguing in Publication Data
A CIP record for this book is available from the British Library

ISBN: 978-1-912508-28-0

This book is also available in the following e-book formats:
MOBI ISBN: 978-1-912508-29-7
EPUB ISBN: 978-1-912508-30-3
Adobe e-book ISBN: 978-1-912508-31-0



Cover design by Out of House Limited
Text design by Greensplash Limited
Project management by Newgen Publishing UK
Printed in the UK by 4edge, Essex

Critical Publishing
3 Connaught Road
St Albans
AL3 5RX

www.criticalpublishing.com

Paper from responsible sources

# Contents

# Meet the authors

Andrew Armitage was head of the department of post-compulsory education at Canterbury Christ Church University and taught in secondary, further, adult and community education and HE for more than 40 years. He was an associate inspector and then Ofsted inspector from 2011 to 2015. He now works as a consultant with universities advising them on teacher training and as a staff developer in the education and training sector. As chair of the Universities' Council for the Education of Teachers (UCET) Post-16 Committee from 2014 to 2017, he was closely involved with the development of the Education and Training Apprenticeships. He is co-author of a number of key texts for FE initial teacher education programmes.

Alison Cogger is currently faculty director of school, college and learning setting partnerships and is the faculty lead on apprenticeships at Canterbury Christ Church University. She completed a vocational qualification in the 1990s and, following her first degree, took a PGCE in post-compulsory education and then taught and acted as a mentor for six years in FE. She worked for the Aim Higher programme, leading on FHE progression, the subject of her Master's dissertation, before moving into adult and community education. She then entered HE as programme director of the PGCE 14–19, which was and remains a nationally unique teacher education programme leading to either QTS or QTLS. She is completing her doctoral thesis on vocational teacher training.

To contact the authors, please do so via their website: www.armitage-et-al.co.uk

# Acknowledgements

The authors and publisher are grateful for the following public sector information which is reproduced free of charge under the Open Government Licence v3.0.

## Chapter 1

Table 1a, Ofqual (2015b) *What Different Qualification Levels Mean: List of Qualification Levels*. Available at: www.gov.uk/what-different-qualification-levels-mean/list-of-qualification-levels (accessed 28 January 2019).

DfE (2018) *Introduction of T Levels*. Policy Paper. Available at: www.gov.uk/government/publications/introduction-of-t-levels/introduction-of-t-levels (accessed 28 January 2019).

Institute for Apprenticeships (2017a) *'How To' Guide for Trailblazers*. Available at: https://dera.ioe.ac.uk/28922 (accessed 28 January 2019).

Table 1b, Institute for Apprenticeships (2015) *Junior Journalist*. Available at: www.instituteforapprenticeships.org/apprenticeship-standards/junior-journalist (accessed 28 January 2019).

Table 1c, Which? University (2018) *The Complete Guide to Higher and Degree Apprenticeships*. London: HMSO. Available at: https://assets.publishing.service.gov.uk/government/uploads/system/uploads/attachment_data/file/706821/Higher_and_degree_apprenticeships_NAS_Which_Uni_Web__25_.pdf (accessed 28 January 2019).

## Chapter 3

Table 3a and Table 3b, descriptors in tables, Institute for Apprenticeships (2017c) *Search the Apprenticeship Standards*. Available at: www.instituteforapprenticeships.org/apprenticeship-standards (accessed 28 January 2019).

Table 3d, Health and Safety Executive, *The Health and Safety Toolbox*. At the time of writing, this was available on the HSE website at: www.hse.gov.uk/pubns/books/hsg268.htm and could be downloaded free.

## Chapter 4

Institute for Apprenticeships (2018) *Assessment Method Guide: Workplace Observation*. Available at: www.instituteforapprenticeships.org/developing-new-apprenticeships/assessment-methods/assessment-method-guide-workplace-observation (accessed 28 January 2019).

## Chapter 5

Paraphrased extract from Institute for Apprenticeships (2017a) *'How To' Guide for Trailblazers*. Available at: https://dera.ioe.ac.uk/28922 (accessed 28 January 2019).

Table 5b, DfE, ETF and AELP (2017) The Future Apprenticeships course 'End-Point Assessment – Prepare to Deliver', *Presentation 6: Professional dialogues as an assessment instrument.*

Paraphrase and project exemplars, Institute for Apprenticeships (2017b) *Assessment Method Guide*. Available at: www.instituteforapprenticeships.org/developing-new-apprenticeships/assessment-methods (accessed 28 January 2019).

Quotation, Institute for Apprenticeships (2017d) *External Quality Assurance*. Available at: www.instituteforapprenticeships.org/quality/external-quality-assurance (accessed 28 January 2019).

# OTHER ACKNOWLEDGEMENTS

## Chapter 2

Geoff Rebbeck for Section 2.8 Current and emerging technologies.

## Chapter 3

The Mentor Development Programme Team, Canterbury Christ Church University, Faculty of Education for Figure 3c The Mentoring Cycle.

## Chapter 4

### Table 4b Competency Framework

The generic competence framework distils findings from: MOSAIC competencies for professional and administrative occupations (US Office of Personnel Management); Spencer and Spencer, Competence at Work; and top performance and leadership competence studies published in Richard H Rosier (ed), *The Competency Model Handbook*, vols 1 and 2 (Boston: Linkage, 1994 and 1995), especially those from Cigna, Sprint, American Express, Sandoz Pharmaceuticals, Wisconsin Power and Light, and Blue Cross and Blue Shield of Maryland. Much of the material comes from *Working with Emotional Intelligence* by Daniel Goleman (London: Bantam, 1998).

The Education and Training Foundation for permission to reproduce the Professional Standards in Table 4e.

Gatsby Foundation for permission to access *Subject Pedagogy for Science, Engineering and Technology Teachers* at: www.gatsby.org.uk/education/programmes/teacher-education-in-FE (accessed 28 January 2019).

## Chapter 5

Paraphrase and quotation, Strategic Development Network (2016) *The Presentation/ Showcase: Under the Bonnet of End-Point Assessment*. Available at: www.strategicdevelopmentnetwork.co.uk/the-showcase-presentation-under-the-bonnet-of-end-point-assessment (accessed 28 January 2019).

# Introduction

*The Richard Review of Apprenticeships* (2012) emphasised the importance of mentoring in the New Apprenticeships:

> *The Government should consider specifying that the employer and apprentice come together at the beginning of the apprenticeship and sign an agreement, setting out what is expected of them. This could include an explicit commitment to work towards the relevant apprenticeship qualification. It should also spell out the training that will be delivered, by whom and where, and the time off work allowed for this. It should be clear who is available to mentor and support the apprentice – in the training organisation and the firm. This is simply good practice, and happens in some cases today. But, going forward, it needs to be a routine part of the approach.*
>
> (Richard, 2012, p 94)

So, although most likely to be a fellow employee of the apprentice, it is possible that you may, as a mentor, be a member of the training provider organisation or its associates. Indeed, any one apprentice may have more than one mentor in the different organisations supporting their apprenticeship. Furthermore, because of this complexity and the varied patterns of off-the-job and on-the-job training, it is possible that you will be acting in other roles with the apprentice – such as trainer for your employer – alongside being a mentor. Despite the importance of the role of the mentor in the New Apprenticeships, training and support for the role has been limited and the aim of this book is to address this.

To further this training and support role, each chapter has a range of learning activities to be carried out yourself, with your apprentice or with other work or training colleagues. There are training and work-based scenarios, prioritisation, ranking, matching or evaluation activities. There are activities that ask you or your apprentice to reflect on your training or experience. There are problem-solving, observation and discussion activities, self-assessment and gapped assessment activities. At the end of each chapter is an action plan which asks you to specify, in relation to key points in the chapter, what your proposed developmental actions will be, who is responsible for these, what the intended target and outcomes are, and the timings for these.

Chapter 1 considers developments and trends in vocational education and training and sets the New Apprenticeships in their historical context. There is a consideration of apprenticeships in modern European countries which, by and large, currently have more effective vocational education and training than the UK. There is an overview of current vocational standards, qualifications and qualification frameworks as well as future developments and their likely impact, particularly the introduction of T levels. There is a consideration of key components of the New Apprenticeships such as the standards and the assessment plan, which sets out the elements of end-point assessment. Finally, there is an account of how degree or higher-level apprenticeships will operate.

The key focus for the mentor/coach is the learning of their apprentice and so Chapter 2 begins with an analysis of the key features of these learners and their learning, particularly of the barriers to learning they may have to overcome. There is an overview of the factors that might affect this learning, such as motivation, ability, age and development. The two dimensions of communication and interaction which should concern the mentor/coach of an apprentice are then described: the first relates to communication *between* the mentor/coach and their apprentice; the second is connected with the apprentice's own communication as part of their occupational role. Although learning theorists offer their own views on how the most effective learning takes place, there is here a consideration of each of their theories, which it is hoped will give apprentices and their mentors, coaches and trainers valuable insights into apprentice learning. Key learning approaches are then set out to illustrate how apprentices may use one or more of a number of preferred approaches to learning in the course of their learning career. After an account of deep and surface learning, there is a consideration of how the nature of organisations might affect learning as well as a view of the importance of current and emerging technologies.

Chapter 3 begins with a focus on your own approach to mentoring before going on to consider your apprentice's likely key learning activities – learning from experience and reflective practice. There is then a characterisation of mentoring as a cyclical process with the major aspects of that process examined, such as target-setting, the recording of learner progress, the managing and maintenance of the mentor–mentee relationship, the qualities of the mentor–mentee relationship and roles, responsibilities and boundaries. After a consideration of the distinction between the mentor and coach there is a focus on the role of safety, health and the environment. There is a discussion of your organisation and your partners in training and the maintenance of your occupational currency and continuous professional development.

Chapter 4 begins by revisiting mentor models and looks at models of coaching, particularly the GROW model. There is a consideration of emotional intelligence with an emphasis on its importance to effective mentoring and coaching and the necessity of building rapport, trust and respect. There is then a focus on the important skills of questioning and listening as well as a consideration of body language or non-verbal communication. There is a consideration of observation skills as well as the teaching, tutoring or instruction activities a mentor/coach may be required to carry out.

Although the end-point assessment of your apprentice will be carried out by an external assessor, your role in preparing your apprentice for this, through formative assessment, will be crucial. Following a consideration of the key features and principles of assessment, Chapter 5 focuses on the key methods currently being used for end-point assessment: portfolio/logbook, professional dialogue, written, verbal or online knowledge test, observed practical assessment, interview or panel discussion, project, presentation or showcase. Finally, there is an overview of the major elements of the quality assurance of assessment and your likely role in relation to it.

# 1 The new apprenticeships

**CHAPTER CONTENT**

This chapter covers:



## 1.1 APPRENTICESHIPS AND TRENDS IN VOCATIONAL EDUCATION AND TRAINING

### Key concepts

In the *Nicomachean Ethics*, Aristotle argues that there are five ways in which '*the soul comes to the truth*'– or, '*five ways of knowing*'. They are:

1. *technique (techné);*
2. *science (episteme);*
3. *practical sense (phronesis);*
4. *wisdom (sophia);*
5. *intelligence (nous).*

(Aristotle, 2011: Book VI, p 3)

These categories do correspond to types of knowledge and understanding that the modern mind would recognise.

- '*Techné*' is art or applied science, most clearly demonstrated in a designer's or architect's ability to create artefacts according to a rational set of rules or principles.

- '*Episteme*' is pure science, the capacity to develop theoretical understanding of natural phenomena, known as natural philosophy in the seventeenth and eighteenth centuries and exemplified in the contemporary study of chemistry, physics and biology.
- '*Phronesis*' represents practical wisdom or intelligence, or how best to act in particular situations. There is also a dimension of ethics and values in '*phronesis*'.
- '*Sophia*' represents theoretical wisdom, a concern with the basic tenets of knowledge and the purest way of knowing.
- '*Nous*' is intelligence, or an innate or intuitive way of knowing.

Most trends in technical education and training have been underpinned by the concepts of techné, phronesis and nous, or a blend of the three.

Gavin Moodie (2002) identifies further key elements of vocational education and training. Vocational education is often associated with certain 'ways of learning', specifically with the vocational learner observing and imitating experienced employees and building up non-verbal or tacit knowledge (nous), or becoming acquainted with a broad field of vocational knowledge in more general vocational preparation programmes. Traditionally, vocational education has been associated with an extrinsic purpose, such as the preparation for work, as opposed to general education's more intrinsic purpose as an end in itself. A similar distinction would suggest that vocational education is training for work directed by others as opposed to general education's emphasis on education as a preparation for more professional, self-directed work.

Finally, Moodie considers vocational education as being distinguished by three hierarchies: occupational level, educational level and cognitive level. With regard to occupational levels, these can be distinguished by skill level, for example, and by occupational role. Moodie cites Stevenson (1992) who '*posited six different skill levels, from the routine proceduralised tasks to management responsibility over others, and eight occupational [role] levels, from operative to senior professional*'. With regard to educational level, vocational qualifications have been offered at a range of educational levels in a variety of frameworks for many years in the UK, as you will see in Sections 1.2 and 1.3 below. The New Apprenticeships have to be levelled and are currently available at levels 1–8 (doctoral level). With regard to cognitive level, Moodie cites Stevenson (1998) who invokes Engestrom's (1994) hierarchy of learning:

> - *first order learning (conditioning, imitation and rote learning);*
> - *second order learning (trial and error or learning by doing and problem-solving, or investigative learning);*
> - *third order learning (questioning and transforming the context or community of practice).*
>
> *This is sometimes mapped to educational levels, with vocational education said to involve first and second order learning and higher education involving second and third order learning.*

## Activity 1

Reflect on your own vocational education and that of your apprentice.

- Which of Aristotle's 'ways of knowing' have you engaged in?
- Which 'ways of learning' have you engaged in?
- How far would you agree that your vocational education and that of your apprentice *has been associated with an extrinsic purpose, such as the preparation for work, as opposed to [a] more intrinsic purpose as an end in itself*?
- How far would you agree that your *vocational education [has been] training for work directed by others as opposed to education as a preparation for more professional, self-directed work*?
- How would you describe your vocational education in terms of its occupational level, educational level and cognitive level?

## Key developments

The Statute of Artificers of 1563 established the seven-year apprenticeship as the model for vocational training in England and craft apprenticeship remained the dominant form of training as far as the Industrial Revolution and beyond, arguably as far as the industrial training legislation of the 1960s. The 50 years since have seen a range of qualifications and initiatives which have sought to introduce occupationally specific training or broader more general programmes of vocational preparation. The year 1973 saw the introduction of the Technician Education Council (TEC) and the Business Education Council (BEC), ten years later to be amalgamated as the Business and Technology Education Council (BTEC) and producing arguably the most successful and durable vocational qualifications of the past 40 years, now offered by the Pearson Group.

Prime Minister James Callaghan initiated the Great Debate about the education of 16–19 year-olds in a speech at Ruskin College, Oxford in 1976. Callaghan expressed real concern about what was offered to this age group and was particularly focused on over-specialisation at A level. Callaghan argued that the goal of education was to equip children to the best of their ability for a lively, constructive place in society and also to fit them to do a job of work. Emphasis should be given to *not one or the other, but both*.

In the late 1970s a concern about the basic skills of young people was precipitated by rising youth unemployment caused by a worsening economic situation both nationally and internationally and addressed by a series of initiatives such as the Youth Opportunities Programme (YOP), the New Training Initiative and YTS (Youth Training Scheme) into the 1980s. The YTS provided off-the-job and on-the-job training as well as training in social and life skills. But the scheme attracted much criticism: '*it provided employment for only two thirds of the trainees who completed the courses and this employment was often short-term*' (Armitage et al, 2016, p 29). Furthermore, the assumption underpinning the YTS – that young people did not have the skills and attitudes to gain employment – suggested its curriculum was based on a deficit model.

In 1983, the Thatcher government embarked on the most ambitious education experiment since the Second World War, this time focusing on the secondary sector: the Technical and Vocational Education Initiative. It was predicated on the belief that secondary education was overly academic and did not equip young people for the world of work. Local authorities were required to form consortia of schools and FE colleges to be eligible for funding to develop a 14+ curriculum that reflected both technical and vocational subjects as well as academic ones.

Perhaps the most dramatic change in direction for vocational education came in 1986 with the establishment of the National Council for Vocational Qualifications. Only 40 per cent of the workforce held relevant vocational qualifications and the UK did not bear comparison with competitor countries. Through the awarding bodies, the NVQ was born. Up until this point, the historical pattern of vocational training had been via day release with a clear dual model of college-based theory and work-based practice and many felt this duality prevented the development of high levels of skills. NVQs were based on National Occupational Standards (NOS), available for almost every role in every sector in the UK. Each unit of an NOS had to comprise:

- a title, reflecting the content of the NOS;
- an overview, an introductory section providing a brief summary of the NOS to help the user judge whether it was relevant to them;
- performance criteria, defining in detail what was expected of the individual;
- underpinning knowledge and understanding, what the individual needed to know and/or understand to enable them to meet the performance criteria;
- scope, specifying the range of circumstances or situations that had a critical impact on the activity when carrying out the performance criteria;
- elements, an NOS was divided into two or more discrete elements that describe the activities the person has to carry out;
- values and behaviours, the personal attributes an individual is expected to demonstrate within the NOS.

This structure, it was believed, removed the distinction between theory and practice by establishing competencies that met performance criteria but also demonstrated underpinning knowledge and values.

Although NVQs have survived to the time of writing, there was some disenchantment with competence-based assessment through the 1990s and 2000s. Armitage et al summarise the sources of this disenchantment:

> *[A leading concern about] competence-based assessment [is related to charges] that it is unable to distinguish between levels of performance. Competences cannot be graded: you are either competent at something or you are not. You cannot be 'very', 'fairly' or 'just about' competent. Critics argue that motivation is*

> *therefore affected; there is simply no incentive for students to strive to do better, when a less thorough performance could be sufficient evidence to gain a 'competence'. Defenders of this approach to assessment point out that it is its avoidance of grading which is its strength; that individual achievement is related to performance criteria and underpinning knowledge rather than being compared to the achievement of other students or some absolute, unattainable standard.*
>
> *The second concern is the extent to which competences focus on the performance or behavioural aspects of learning, rather than, say, cognitive aspects which are not so easily demonstrable publicly. While some may be happy with this focus for more obviously skill-based learning, it is argued that its application is inappropriate to professional contexts which require greater knowledge and understanding, such as nurse education, social work training, teacher education or police training.*
>
> (Armitage et al, 2016, p 172)

General National Vocational Qualifications (GNVQs) were introduced in 1992 and had a shelf life of 15 years. Unlike NVQs, which were meant to be work-based, GNVQs were intended for use in schools and colleges. Like NVQs, the assessment of GNVQs was evidence-based and the emphasis was very much on coursework designed to provide the evidence for the successful meeting of performance criteria. GNVQs were offered at Foundation, Intermediate and Advanced levels and successful candidates achieved either a pass, a merit or a distinction. GNVQs were relatively successful and by 1997, those with Advanced GNVQs were more likely to gain a university place, particularly on certain vocational degrees, than those with A levels.

James Mirza-Davies traces the development of Modern Apprenticeships from their announcement in 1993:

> *[They were] rolled out over the following two years. Modern Apprentices would count as employees and be paid a wage, with a written agreement between employers and apprentices. Modern apprentices were required to work towards an NVQ level 3 qualification, equivalent to A-levels today. Shortly afterwards, National Traineeships were introduced at level 2, equivalent to GCSEs. These were intended as 'a progression route into apprenticeships for those young people who were not ready to enter a level three programme.' By the end of 1998, under the Labour Government 1997–2010, almost a quarter of a million people in England and Wales had started a Modern Apprenticeship. The most popular sectors were business administration, engineering and retailing. The majority of employers were small firms and there were very few employers with more than five apprentices. The Modern Apprenticeship system continued to evolve with National Traineeships becoming Foundation Modern Apprenticeships and 'Modern Apprenticeships' becoming 'Advanced Modern Apprenticeships.' In the early 2000s national frameworks were introduced defining the minimum standards required for each apprenticeship. In 2004, Advanced Modern Apprenticeships become 'Advanced Apprenticeships' and Foundation Modern Apprenticeships become simply 'Apprenticeships' (these would later be rebranded again as 'Intermediate Apprenticeships'). At the same time the upper age limit of 25 was removed and pre-apprenticeships were introduced for people not ready to enter a*

*full apprenticeship. Young apprenticeships were also introduced for 14–16 year olds still in school.*

(Mirza-Davies, 2015)

The next major development in vocational education was to be vocational diplomas, which took various forms over nearly a decade but were first announced in the 2002 Green Paper *14–19: Extending Opportunities, Raising Standards.* Among key proposals were a matriculation diploma recognising students' achievement at 19 as well as the introduction of work-related courses from 14.

This was followed up in 2004 by the *Tomlinson Report.* Tomlinson proposed replacing GCSEs and A levels with diplomas that would cover both academic and vocational disciplines. The Blair government did not implement the *Tomlinson Report*: some commentators felt that, in an election year, the abandonment of the gold standard of GCSE and A level was too much of a risk for them to take.

The government commissioned the *Leitch Report on Skills* (DfES, 2006), which had some specific recommendations on apprenticeships, including increasing the number of apprenticeships to 500,000 per year by 2020 (in the UK). The report noted that there had been some increase in participation but highlighted low completion rates and a view from employers that the process was complex and bureaucratic. Leitch proposed that '*the Government should consider creating a new entitlement as resources allow so that every young person with the right qualifications should be able to take up an Apprenticeship place*', and that employers should drive the content of apprenticeships through their Sector Skills Council.

Alison Wolf's report *Review of Vocational Education* (Wolf, 2011) made 27 recommendations, and among those relating to apprenticeships and technical education were:

- *The overall study programmes of all 16–18 year-olds in 'vocational' programmes (i.e. currently everything other than A levels, pre-U and IB, and including 'Foundation Learning') should be governed by a set of general principles relating primarily to content, general structure, assessment arrangements and contact time.*
- *Students who are under 19 and do not have GCSE A*–C in English and/or Maths should be required, as part of their programme, to pursue a course which either leads directly to these qualifications, or which provide significant progress towards future GCSE entry and success.*
- *The DfE and BIS should evaluate the extent to which the current general education components of apprenticeship frameworks are adequate for 16–19 year old apprentices, many of whom may wish to progress to further and higher education.*
- *At present teachers with QTS can teach in FE colleges; the FE equivalent – QTLS – should be recognised in schools, which is currently not the case. This will enable schools to recruit qualified professionals to teach courses at school level (rather than bussing pupils to colleges) with clear efficiency gains.*

In 2012, the government commissioned Doug Richard to, in his own words, '*answer [the] question: What should an apprenticeship be in the future, and how can apprenticeships meet the needs of the changing economy?*' (Richard, 2012, p 2). His key recommendations were:

1. *Apprenticeships should be redefined. They should be clearly targeted at those who are new to a job or role that requires sustained and substantial training.*
2. *The focus of apprenticeships should be on the outcome.*
3. *The Government should set up a contest for the best qualification. Individual employers, employer partnerships or other organisations with the relevant expertise should be invited to design and develop apprenticeship qualifications for their sectors.*
4. *The testing and validation process should be independent and genuinely respected by industry.*
5. *All apprentices should have achieved Level 2 in English and maths before they can complete their apprenticeship. Maths and English taught within apprenticeships should be sufficiently functional in approach to be suitable for an apprenticeship context.*
6. *The Government should encourage diversity and innovation in delivering apprenticeships. There will be many paths and approaches that an apprentice can take to reach 'the standard' and we should strip out any unnecessary prescription and regulation of the process for getting there.*
7. *The Government has a role in promoting good quality delivery.*
8. *Government funding must create the right incentives for apprenticeship training. The purchasing power for investing in apprenticeship training should lie with the employer. Government should contribute to the cost, but this should be routed via the employer, in order to ensure relevance and drive up quality.*
9. *Learners and employers need access to good quality information.*
10. *Government must actively boost awareness of the new apprenticeship model.*

(Richard, 2012, p 17)

Since 2015 young people have been required to continue in learning or training until age 18. Raising the participation age (RPA) has not meant young people must stay in school. They can choose one of the following options:

- Full-time education, such as school, college or home education.
- Apprenticeships, work-based learning.
- Part-time education or training if they are employed, self-employed or volunteering for at least 20 hours a week.

### Activity 2

- From what you have read above about developments in vocational education and apprenticeships, are there any that have been important for your vocational/professional development or that of your apprentice?

## Lessons from abroad: international comparisons

Vocational education and training (VET) in England is often unfavourably compared with that in other countries. In many countries, VET is an important element of upper secondary education, whereas our current government's policies have sought to restrict VET to post-16 contexts. In Germany, students can enrol for the upper stage of secondary education in *Berufsschulen* (vocational schools). Students can pursue programmes either full-time in the schools themselves or can enter the dual system, which combines part-time study and work-based training. Much is made of the Meister system, which requires trainers to be both master craftspeople and highly qualified teachers. In France, after lower secondary education, students can enrol for a year in a general and technological *lycée* or vocational *lycée*. This integration of vocational and general education suggests that the vocational versus academic divide that has afflicted English education is not present elsewhere, and that a firm foundation for further VET is laid in the secondary phase.

At present, overseas apprenticeships are longer and involve more general education than existing English apprenticeships:

> *[English apprenticeships last] an average of 18 months, compared with 3–4 years in some other countries. English apprentices therefore commonly spend less time in total education and training than those in many other countries. A 3- or 4-year apprenticeship in Denmark, Norway, Austria, Switzerland or Germany will involve a substantial amount of general education, provided off the job – this may be of the order of 400 hours. This contrasts with the English and maths requirements in an English apprenticeship, which are primarily remedial, and if they apply will involve only around 50 hours of study.*
>
> (Kuczera and Field, 2018, p 12)

There are a number of key features of the New Apprenticeships that will lead to their closer alignment with those in other countries:

- There will be one apprenticeship standard for each occupational role.
- The standards comprise detailed specifications of required knowledge, skills and behaviours, which have been devised by groups of employer-led groups.
- In Canada, Germany, Norway and Switzerland, for example, there are high standards for workplace apprentice supervisors, which need to be emulated in England.

# 1.2 VOCATIONAL STANDARDS, QUALIFICATIONS AND QUALIFICATION FRAMEWORKS: T LEVELS AND THE FUTURE

## Vocational standards, qualifications and qualification frameworks

Since 2015, qualifications have had to meet the requirements of the Regulated Qualifications Framework (RQF), overseen by the government's qualification watchdog, Ofqual. The RQF

> *provides a single, simple system for cataloguing all qualifications regulated by [Ofqual]. It's like a bookcase in a library, with qualifications indexed by their 'level' and 'size'. Qualifications at any specific level can be very different from one another, for example in their content and purpose. [Ofqual] maintains a register that provides more detail on each qualification (alpharegister.ofqual.gov.uk).*
>
> *Qualification Levels indicate the difficulty and complexity of the knowledge and skills associated with any qualification. There are eight levels supported by three 'entry' levels. While most qualifications will be assigned a single level some, such as GCSEs, can span more than one.*
>
> *Qualification Size refers to the estimated total amount of time it could typically take to study and be assessed for a qualification. This can be anything from a matter of hours to several years of study and different students can take different amounts of time to study for the same qualification. Size is expressed in terms of Total Qualification Time (TQT). The part of that time typically spent being taught or supervised, rather than studying alone, is known as Guided Learning Hours.*
>
> *Qualifications can sit at different levels, but require similar amounts of study and assessment time. Equally, qualifications at the same level can take different amounts of study and assessment time.*
>
> *The RQF replaced the Qualifications and Credit Framework, and National Qualifications Framework.*
>
> (Ofqual, 2015a)

The RQF for England, Wales and Northern Ireland has nine qualification levels as shown in Table 1a.

*Table 1a Regulated Qualifications Framework*

| **Entry level** |
|---|
| Each entry level qualification is available at three sub-levels – 1, 2 and 3. Entry level 3 is the most difficult.<br>Entry level qualifications are:<br>• entry level award<br>• entry level certificate (ELC)<br>• entry level diploma<br>• entry level English for speakers of other languages (ESOL)<br>• entry level essential skills<br>• entry level functional skills<br>• Skills for Life |
| **Level 1**<br>Level 1 qualifications are:<br>• first certificate<br>• GCSE – grades 3, 2, 1 or grades D, E, F, G<br>• level 1 award<br>• level 1 certificate<br>• level 1 diploma<br>• level 1 ESOL<br>• level 1 essential skills<br>• level 1 functional skills<br>• level 1 national vocational qualification (NVQ)<br>• music grades 1, 2 and 3 |
| **Level 2**<br>Level 2 qualifications are:<br>• CSE – grade 1<br>• GCSE – grades 9, 8, 7, 6, 5, 4 or grades A*, A, B, C<br>• intermediate apprenticeship<br>• level 2 award<br>• level 2 certificate<br>• level 2 diploma<br>• level 2 ESOL<br>• level 2 essential skills<br>• level 2 functional skills<br>• level 2 national certificate<br>• level 2 national diploma<br>• level 2 NVQ |

- music grades 4 and 5
- level – grade A, B or C

**Level 3**

Level 3 qualifications are:

- A level
- access to higher education diploma
- advanced apprenticeship
- applied general
- AS level
- international Baccalaureate diploma
- level 3 award
- level 3 certificate
- level 3 diploma
- level 3 ESOL
- level 3 national certificate
- level 3 national diploma
- level 3 NVQ
- music grades 6, 7 and 8
- tech level

**Level 4**

Level 4 qualifications are:

- certificate of higher education (Cert HE)
- higher apprenticeship
- higher national certificate (HNC)
- level 4 award
- level 4 certificate
- level 4 diploma
- level 4 NVQ

**Level 5**

Level 5 qualifications are:

- diploma of higher education (DipHE)
- foundation degree
- higher national diploma (HND)
- level 5 award
- level 5 certificate
- level 5 diploma
- level 5 NVQ

| **Level 6** |
|---|
| Level 6 qualifications are:<br>• degree apprenticeship<br>• degree with honours – for example Bachelor of the Arts (BA) Hons, Bachelor of Science (BSc) Hons<br>• graduate certificate<br>• graduate diploma<br>• level 6 award<br>• level 6 certificate<br>• level 6 diploma<br>• level 6 NVQ<br>• ordinary degree without honours |
| **Level 7** |
| Level 7 qualifications are:<br>• integrated Master's degree, for example Master of Engineering (MEng)<br>• level 7 award<br>• level 7 certificate<br>• level 7 diploma<br>• level 7 NVQ<br>• Master's degree, for example Master of Arts (MA), Master of Science (MSc)<br>• postgraduate certificate<br>• postgraduate certificate in education (PGCE)<br>• postgraduate diploma |
| **Level 8** |
| Level 8 qualifications are:<br>• doctorate, for example doctor of philosophy (PhD or DPhil)<br>• level 8 award<br>• level 8 certificate<br>• level 8 diploma |

(Ofqual, 2015b)

## *Activity 3*

Consider the vocational qualifications you have taken (or their current equivalent) as well as any your apprentice is engaged in.

- What level are they and what are their key features (module structure, attendance pattern, guided learning hours (GLH))?

## T levels and the future

Lord Sainsbury's Independent Panel on Technical Education reported in April 2016 (DfE/BIS, 2016a). Among its recommendations, all of which were accepted by the government, were:

- *The Government develops a coherent technical education option which develops the technical knowledge and skills required to enter skilled employment, which leads from levels 2/3 to levels 4/5 and beyond, and which is highly valued because it works in the marketplace*
- *The technical education option should be recognised as having two modes of learning: employment-based (typically an apprenticeship) and college based.*
- *A single, common framework of standards should cover both apprenticeships and college-based provision.*
- *The development of short, flexible bridging provision to enable individuals to move, in either direction, between the academic and technical education options and to support adults returning to study.*
- *A common framework of 15 routes is established which encompasses all employment-based and college-based technical education at levels 2 to 5. These would be:*
    1. *Agriculture, Environmental and Animal Care*
    2. *Business and Administrative*
    3. *Catering and Hospitality*
    4. *Childcare and Education*
    5. *Construction*
    6. *Creative and Design*
    7. *Digital*
    8. *Engineering and Manufacturing*
    9. *Hair and Beauty*
    10. *Health and Science*
    11. *Legal, Finance and Accounting*
    12. *Protective Services*
    13. *Sales, Marketing and Procurement*
    14. *Social Care*
    15. *Transport and Logistics*
- *The Government moves away from the current awarding organisation market model, where qualifications which deliver similar but different outcomes compete with one another, and instead adopts a licensing approach. Any technical*

*education qualification at levels 2 and 3 should be offered and awarded by a single body or consortium, under a licence covering a fixed period of time following an open competition*

- *The Government undertakes further work to examine how to ensure clear progression routes develop from levels 4 and 5 to degree apprenticeships and other higher education at levels 6 and 7.*
- *Every college based route should begin with a two-year programme suitable for 16–18 year olds*
- *There is a single set of maths and English 'exit' requirements governing college based technical education and apprenticeships. These should be seen as the minimum level of maths or English which all individuals must achieve ahead of securing technical education certification, as is already the case for apprentices.*
- *In addition to work taster or short-duration work experience opportunities in their first year, every 16–18 year old student following a two-year college-based technical education programme should be entitled to a high-quality, structured work placement.*

The most important outcome of the Sainsbury report and the government's subsequent *Post-16 Skills Plan* (DfE/BIS, 2016b) has arguably been the development of T levels (not to be confused with the Tech Level, which is an existing level 3 qualification, nor the 'TechBacc', which requires students to achieve a Tech Level qualification, a level 3 maths qualification and an extended project qualification), regarded as a twin track to the traditional academic A level route.

## T levels

From 2020, T levels will give students aged 16 to 18 a technical alternative to A levels and will help them to get a skilled job. T levels will provide a mixture of technical knowledge and practical skills specific to their chosen industry or occupation, an industry placement of at least 45 days in their chosen industry or occupation, relevant maths, English and digital skills, and common workplace skills.

T levels will offer students a mixture of classroom or workshop-based learning and 'on-the-job' experience.

At the time of writing, it was intended that T levels would be phased in starting from the 2020–21 academic year with a small number of providers. The very first T level subjects will be taught from September 2020 in more than 50 colleges and other education and training providers, which means children who entered Year 10 in September 2018 will be the first to be able to study them.

The first subjects that can be studied in 2020 will be digital, construction, and education and childcare.

T levels will become one of three main options when a student reaches the age of 16, alongside:

- apprenticeships for students who wish to learn a specific occupation 'on the job';
- A levels for students who wish to continue academic education.

It has been recognised that the current range of technical qualifications is confusing and that some have been more successful than others. T levels will simplify choices for post-16 technical education for students, parents and providers. Both T levels and apprenticeships will be based on the same standards for their relevant occupations, approved by the Institute for Apprenticeships (IfA).

The subject range of T level programmes will be defined by the IfA's occupational maps.

Groups of employers define the skills and requirements for T levels for each industry by participating in 'T level panels'. Total time for a T level is expected to be around 1,800 hours over two years (including the industry placement of at least 45 days). This is a significant increase over most current technical education programmes.

T level programmes will include three mandatory elements:

- core underpinning theories, concepts and workplace skills, tailored for their chosen industry or occupation;
- occupationally specialist skills;
- an industry placement with an employer, which will last for at least 45 working days.

The 'core' will be split into two parts.

- One part will develop 'underpinning' technical knowledge and skills relevant to all occupations relevant to the T level's industry. This will require students to:
  - understand how the industry works;
  - understand how occupational specialisms fit within the industry;
  - know what the working practices in the industry are like.
- The other part is an employer-set project that will require students to apply their core knowledge and skills to achieve an employer-set challenge or brief.

Industry or occupational specialisms will be based on the same standards as apprenticeships. For T levels, these skills will be delivered in a 'classroom-based' environment (including, for example, workshops and simulated working environments).

T levels must contain a meaningful industry placement with an employer. These will last a minimum of 45 working days, but can last up to 60 working days.

## *Activity 4*

Not all commentators have welcomed the prospect of T levels. Fiona Millar writes in *The Guardian*:

> *In the subsequent 15 years (since Sir Mike Tomlinson's inquiry) we have had Ed Balls's short-lived diplomas and the Wolf review of vocational education, which rightly abolished a swathe of meaningless qualifications. The most recent investigation by Lord Sainsbury led to the plan for 15 'world class' alternatives to academic routes. The twin-track approach will include T-levels – classroom-based training programmes – and work-based apprenticeships, whose numbers appear to be plunging already.*
>
> *Meanwhile GCSEs and A-levels are still standing and remain the qualification of choice in a financial climate where FE colleges are underfunded, schools must fight ferociously to retain their post-16 students and there are questions over the quality and availability of suitable teaching staff for the new wave of technical study.*
>
> *Like many others I sincerely hope this latest heave works, but I suspect we will be having the same conversation about technical education in 10 years' time. Nothing about the T-level/apprenticeships route convinces that the parity of esteem issue will be overcome – maybe only a baccalaureate-style qualification can do this?*
>
> (Millar, 2018)

- In the light of your discussion in Activity 3 above about your own vocational qualification and that of your apprentice, are T levels to be welcomed or, as Millar anticipates, will they not provide the answer for high level technical education?

# 1.3 THE ROLE OF THE TRAILBLAZERS: THE STANDARDS AND THE ASSESSMENT PLAN

## The trailblazers and the standards

Trailblazer groups are responsible for developing the standards and assessment plans for individual apprenticeships. Each group has a wide range of at least ten different employers. They should reflect the range of companies that employ people in this occupation – including size, geographical spread and sector.

The Institute for Apprenticeships sets out the requirements for standards (Institute for Apprenticeships, 2017a). They are expressed in terms of knowledge, skills and behaviours. They should:

- be short, concise and clear;
- set out the full competence needed in an occupation;
- ensure that, upon completing the apprenticeship, someone should be able to carry out the role in any size of employer and in any relevant sector;
- contain a clear occupational profile setting out the responsibilities of the occupation and linked to the knowledge, skills and behaviours that will be applied in the workplace;
- have the support of employers, including smaller businesses – this means that a wide range of employers must be involved in development of the standard, recognise it as fit for purpose and have signed up to use it;
- contain sufficient breadth and depth and be pitched at such a level that a new entrant to the occupation will find it stretching – it should require at least one year of training (before the end-point assessment) with at least 20 per cent of the employment being off-the-job training;
- align with professional registration where it exists – where there is professional registration, the apprenticeship standard should provide someone with the knowledge, skills and experience they need to be eligible to apply for this;
- contain minimum English and maths requirements and any digital skills required; either at the minimum level set by government for all apprentices or above the minimum level if the trailblazer group thinks this is appropriate. The current minimum government English and maths requirements are:
  - for level 2 apprenticeships, achieve level 1 English and maths and take the test for level 2 prior to taking their end-point assessment;
  - for level 3 to 8 apprenticeships, achieve level 2 English and maths prior to taking their end-point assessment.
- only include mandatory qualifications under certain circumstances. Degree apprenticeships are not covered by this rule, since the qualification is an integral element of the apprenticeship.

## *Activity 5*

- Table 1b shows the approved standard for a junior journalist level 3 (Institute for Apprenticeships, 2015). Consider how far this standard meets the criteria above.

*Table 1b Junior journalist level 3*

**Overview of the role**

Creating news items using a combination of words, pictures and moving images.

**Details of standard**

**1. Job**

Junior journalist

**2. Duration**

We would expect a candidate coming onto this apprenticeship, without previous relevant experience, to typically take at least 18 months to complete the programme. This may be reduced if an apprentice is part-qualified or has relevant experience on entry.

**3. Role profile**

Journalists bring people the news and information from their street, their community, their town or city and from around the world using a combination of words, pictures and moving images. They are able to work on their own competently and work without immediate supervision in generating and producing stories for publication and/or broadcast. At the successful completion of this apprenticeship, you will become a junior journalist.

**4. Knowledge and skills**

Journalists will use their knowledge and skills to produce news and information for TV, radio, print and digital publications. These are the core skills for a junior journalist:

- know what a story is and how to carry out the necessary research and interviews;
- build and maintain a range of reliable contacts;
- create quality stories that are accurate, clear, vigorous, fair and balanced, in a form that will engage an audience;
- work in an ethical manner and in accordance with relevant codes of conduct and demonstrate integrity;
- be able to work on getting stories 'right the first time';
- demonstrate an ability to write and use good English to industry standard for all platforms;
- produce content for digital platforms, including video and photographic material;
- adept at using social media and digital platforms and techniques to source content, contacts and build an audience;
- be a good communicator;
- understand the importance and value of brands;
- connect with the audience they serve;
- work to tight deadlines;
- be technically proficient and able to understand/use web analytics;
- understand how society works;
- take and keep accurate notes and records;
- be able to gather, verify and make proper use of User Generated Content (UGC);

- be able to gather, use and present data;
- understand how the law affects the work of a journalist;
- adhere to relevant health and safety legislation in the workplace; and
- understand the 'news business' with a knowledge of emerging trends in the media industry.

Apprentices will follow one of the following pathways to gain the additional specialist skills:

**For print and associated digital platforms, journalists must:**

- for most employers, write and accurately transcribe shorthand at 100 words per minute;
- edit copy and write headlines for publication on different platforms;
- take photographs suitable for publication;
- be able to report from a wide range of settings;
- research and write clear, accurate, compliant and engaging stories and features for newspapers, magazines and websites;
- for some employers, be able to use data to contribute towards potential editorial content and strategies; and have a good working knowledge of regulation as laid out in the editors' code.

**For TV/radio and associated digital platforms, journalists must:**

- research and write clear, accurate, balanced, compliant and engaging stories for TV and radio;
- for some employers, be able to write and accurately transcribe shorthand at 100 words per minute;
- understand the techniques of interviewing for broadcast and can conduct a simple broadcast interview themselves;
- demonstrate familiarity with the basic techniques and technology of broadcast news gathering, including the sourcing of material;
- have an awareness of the basic set-up of radio and television news studios, operate simple radio and television equipment, and be familiar with the language and terminology of a broadcast newsroom;
- show a good working knowledge of the key principles of broadcast regulation as laid out in the Ofcom Broadcasting Code; and BBC editorial guidelines.

**For public relations (PR), corporate communications and associated digital platforms, journalists must:**

- understand how journalism in PR and corporate communications differs from journalism in other sectors;
- for some employers, be able to write and accurately transcribe shorthand at 100 words per minute;
- be able to prepare content for specific purposes (eg, press releases, social media, brochures, exhibition boards);
- have a good understanding of the business (businesses) they work for;
- know the difference between outputs (eg, press releases, social media etc); and
- be able to act as a mediator and facilitator between the media and employer.

**Qualities**

Journalists should have: a hard-working attitude; an inquiring mind; a lively interest in current affairs; an ability to write and use words accurately and with effect; persistence and determination; and a willingness to embrace change and accept unsocial working hours. They must be able to demonstrate commitment and desire to be a journalist. They must have professional attitudes to their job, how they present themselves for work and have an understanding of the diversity of their audience. They should also be: prepared to work shifts; conscientious; enthusiastic; resilient; a team player; have an ability and desire to carry out duties in accordance with the law, regulations and any appropriate codes of conduct; and have high personal standards in terms of discretion/confidentiality.

### *Activity 6*

- Identify five items of knowledge and skills and five behaviours you would deem essential to be included in the standard for your apprentice.
- Then, on the Institute for Apprenticeship's website www.instituteforapprenticeships.org/apprenticeship-standards, locate the approved standard that is the closest to your apprenticeship.
- How far were the items of knowledge, skills and qualities you identified reflected in that standard?

## End-point assessment and the assessment plan

Key recommendations from the *Richard Review* (2012) were that the focus of apprenticeships should be on the outcome and that the testing and validation process should be independent and genuinely respected by industry. Accordingly, in order to successfully complete an apprenticeship, the apprentice must pass the end-point assessment. This is specified in an assessment plan developed by the trailblazer group and assessed by an independent registered end-point assessor. This aspect of the New Apprenticeships was meant to remove any of the shortcomings of on-course assessment and standardise the point at which trainees were judged to be 'job ready'. Some see this as a parallel to the reforms of GCSEs and A levels with their increased emphasis on summative assessment.

*The assessment plan must lead to an assessment which:*

- *provides robust and holistic assessment;*
- *uses a range of appropriate assessment methods;*
- *includes an appropriate grading;*

- *produces consistent and reliable judgements*
- *is appropriate to the level and proportionate to the planned length of the apprenticeship;*
- *is manageable and feasible for employers of all sizes;*
- *includes professional body recognition (where applicable).*

(Institute for Apprenticeships, 2017a)

## *Activity 7*

Consider the assessment plan for the junior journalist at: www.instituteforapprenticeships.org/media/1070/junior_journalist.pdf

- How far is it an effective assessment of the standards for this apprenticeship set out above?
- To what extent does it meet the criteria for what an assessment plan must lead to above?

Then look at the assessment plan for the apprenticeship standard you considered in Activity 6.

- How far is it an effective assessment of the standards for this apprenticeship?
- To what extent does it meet the criteria for what an assessment plan must lead to above?

We take a more detailed look at the assessment of apprenticeships in Chapter 5.

## 1.4 HIGHER AND DEGREE APPRENTICESHIPS

Higher- and degree-level apprenticeships are for employees aged 18 years or over. These apprenticeships provide alternatives to traditional study at university.

For organisations providing higher- and degree-level apprenticeships, the requirements remain the same as for levels 2 and 3 in that the organisation is required to register as a provider of apprenticeships on the Register of Apprenticeship Training Providers (RoATP). For further education colleges (FECs) and other training providers this may be familiar ground, but for universities in general it is new territory. There are stringent rules for universities providing apprenticeships and these relate to qualification levels. As a training provider, a university is able to provide level 4 and level 5 apprenticeships – known as higher-level apprenticeships – and level 6 and level 7 – known as degree or degree-level apprenticeships. Together they are known as HDAs (higher and degree apprenticeships).

At the time of writing, there are anomalies: for example, the Teacher Apprenticeship at level 6 is not a degree nor does it contain any academic credit – however, it is graduate entry only and so teacher apprentices will find themselves working at a level at which they have already achieved.

These apprenticeships are similar in nature to apprenticeships at levels 2–3 in that they combine working with studying for a work-based qualification. Apprentices will work towards completing a government-approved apprenticeship scheme, a vocational training programme lasting at least 12 months. Higher- and degree-level apprentices can be existing or new employees in any organisation. They must also be paid at least the minimum wage during their apprenticeship. This does not necessarily mean the lowest wage but more likely a wage or salary commensurate to the post. For example, if undertaking an apprenticeship in policing, then an apprentice would be paid the same as a trainee police officer following any other training programme.

As with apprenticeships at levels 2 and 3, each apprenticeship is governed by the apprenticeship standard and must be approved by the Institute for Apprenticeships. The standard for each occupational role will have been developed for use by a national driven trailblazer group and identify the knowledge, skills and behaviours required of each job or occupational role and the end-point assessment (EPA) for each of these roles. If an apprenticeship standard contains an academic degree, at least two higher education institutions must be involved in its development.

- Higher and degree apprenticeships are available at levels 4–8.
- Trainees will combine work with study and will include a work-based, academic or combined qualification or a professional qualification relevant to the industry.
- Levels 4 and 5 are equivalent to a higher education certificate/diploma or a foundation degree level. Level 6 is equivalent to a Bachelor's degree level and level 7 is equivalent to a Master's-level study.
- The skills, knowledge and behaviours of an apprenticeship will be mapped to the learning outcomes of high-quality university-validated programmes as soon as the standard is developed and approved for use. There is a link to professional registration where professional registration exists.
- A higher-level apprentice can study part-time at a college or university or with a training provider.
- Apprenticeships take between one and five (or it can be seven) years to complete.

*Table 1c Examples of higher- and degree-level apprenticeships*

| STANDARDS | LEVEL | STANDARDS | LEVEL |
|---|---|---|---|
| Actuarial Technician | 4 | Healthcare Science Associate | 4 |
| Advanced Dairy Technologist | 5 | Insurance Professional | 4 |
| Aerospace Engineer | 6 | Investment Operations Specialist | 4 |
| Aerospace Software Development Engineer | 6 | Junior 2D Artist (visual effects) | 4 |
| Aircraft Maintenance Certifying Engineer | 4 | Junior Management Consultant | 4 |
| Assistant Technical Director (visual effects) | 4 | Laboratory Scientist | 5 |
| Associate Ambulance Practitioner | 4 | Licensed Conveyancer | 6 |
| Associate Project Manager | 4 | Manufacturing Engineer | 6 |
| Aviation Operations Manager | 4 | Network Engineer | 4 |
| Bespoke Tailor and Cutter | 5 | Nuclear Scientist and Nuclear Engineer | 6 |
| Bus and Coach Engineering Manager | 4 | Nuclear Welding Inspection Technician | 4 |
| Chartered Legal Executive | 6 | Operations/Departmental Manager | 5 |
| Chartered Manager | 6 | Outside Broadcasting Engineer | 7 |
| Chartered Surveyor | 6 | Paraplanner | 4 |
| Control/Technical Support Engineer | 6 | Product Design and Development Engineer | 6 |
| Conveyancing Technician | 4 | Professional Accounting Taxation Technician | 4 |
| Cyber Intrusion Analyst | 4 | Public Sector Commercial Professional | 4 |
| Cyber Security Technologist | 4 | Rail Engineering Advanced Technician | 4 |
| Data Analyst | 4 | Relationship Manager (Banking) | 6 |
| Dental Practice Manager | 4 | Retail Manager | 4 |
| Dental Technician | 5 | Senior Compliance/Risk Specialist | 6 |
| Digital and Technology Solutions Professional | 6 | Senior Housing/Property Management | 4 |
| Electrical/Electronic Technical Support Engineer | 6 | Software Developer | 4 |
| Electrical Power Protection and Plant Commissioning Engineer | 4 | Software Tester | 4 |
| Embedded Electronic Systems Design and Development | 6 | Solicitor | 7 |
| Financial Adviser | 4 | Systems Engineering | 7 |
| Healthcare Assistant Practitioner | 5 | Unified Communications Trouble Shooter | 4 |

From Which? University, 2018

The process for undertaking an apprenticeship will often be through a recruitment and selection process even when it involves internal organisations' current employees. It can be competitive. The employer signs a contract with the higher education institution and agrees to the apprentice having 20 per cent off the job training. Entry requirements for each apprenticeship standard can be found at www.gov.uk/government/collections/apprenticeship-standards. There may also be additional requirements concerned with, for example, safeguarding, and entrants to apprenticeship programmes must satisfy the requirements for clearance related to criminal convictions and working with vulnerable people. When this is the case, employers are required to undertake these checks in a similar way to any other employee. Some apprenticeships will require experience of working in another organisation (for example, health and education professional training generally require this) and apprenticeship programme arrangements for safeguarding between employers will be specified beforehand. There will also be 'right to work' status checks undertaken by the employer.

## End-point assessment including underlying academic awards

The apprentice should be thoroughly tested against the criteria related to the standard before they complete their apprenticeship. To ensure that the testing is fair and rigorous, it must be done by an independent third party that has not been involved in the employment or training of the apprentice.

Apprenticeship providers will have higher and degree-awarding powers and as such are quality-assured in two ways: currently, inspecting higher-level apprenticeships at levels 4 and 5 is the responsibility of Ofsted using the FE Learning and Skills Framework. For example, an apprenticeship for the Nursing Associate with a foundation degree at level 5 is monitored and inspected by Ofsted. Apprenticeships at level 6 and above come under the scrutiny of the Quality Assurance Agency.

Many apprenticeships at higher levels will have mandatory qualifications as outcomes of the apprenticeship. For example, the Chartered Manager Degree apprenticeship has been one of the most popular routes utilised by employers to upskill their existing managers. This has attracted some criticism as some organisations have been swift to use their levy money on current staff and not on creating new employee positions. There has also been some criticism of the value of the degree apprenticeship. David Allison, reporting in *FE Week* in October 2017, points out that the status of some of the providers of these apprenticeships are dubious with, he claims, one provider registered to a flat in London (Allison, 2017).

Approval of apprenticeship programmes in HEIs is through two different ways and this will be dependent on the requirements of an individual apprenticeship standard.

> *It may utilise an existing programme of study that does not integrate Apprenticeship Standards (or validate one especially, either prior to or concurrently but separately from the approval of the Apprenticeship Standards) and approve additionally the Apprenticeship training requirements and the means of assessing the occupational competences that enable the Apprenticeship to be awarded (where the*

> *underlying academic qualification is awarded prior to the End-Point assessment). It may validate a fully integrated degree course specifically for apprentices, which delivers and assesses both the Academic Programme and the Apprenticeship Standards (where the underlying academic qualification is awarded as part of the End-Point assessment).*
>
> (Canterbury Christ Church University, 2018)

Validation processes include an approval event to ensure that the rules of the IfA have been met. This ensures:

- that the employer has co-designed the curriculum;
- that all elements of the apprenticeship standard are covered by the programme;
- that the apprenticeship programme prepares the apprentice for the end-point assessment – and the EPA organisation has been chosen;
- viability of the apprenticeship programme (linked to funding bands).

It is important to consider carefully the higher education institution awarding any qualification as part of or a mandatory element of an apprenticeship. Degree apprenticeships, like other apprenticeships, are developed in partnership with employers, universities and professional bodies. There are other considerations for degree apprenticeships such as the university providers' Regulation and Credit Frameworks, which outline the rules and regulations around degree awards generally, but these should also be read in conjunction with the apprenticeship standard and any other elements required for preparation through 'the Gateway'.

## Mentoring

If you are a mentor, you will be supporting your apprentice(s) who may be undertaking an apprenticeship with an underlying academic award (L4, L5, L6, L7 or L8). These awards may be, for example, a foundation degree (as with Nurse Associates), a sector-specific certificate or diploma (the Diploma in Education & Training in the Learning and Skills Teacher), a part of a degree apprenticeship, such as the Chartered Manager Degree Apprenticeship, or the MBA, MA or MSc in Senior Leadership Apprenticeships. Some of these apprenticeships may be studied on a part-time basis while in full-time employment.

### *Activity 8*

Consider your own CPD in your industry sector and how you progressed to your current role.

- How were you recruited to your role?
- Does your current role have professional registration as a requirement?

## *Activity 9*

- Does the apprenticeship you are mentoring for have alignment with professional registration as part of the apprenticeship standard?
- Does the apprenticeship standard have an academic award?
- What opportunities are there for your apprentice to progress in your organisation?
- How does your organisation promote learners' progression – does it focus on skills needed, employability and social mobility, for example?
- Is there a progression map for staff engaging in apprenticeships? If not, are you able to develop one?

You may be a mentor in an organisation that is registered as a provider and your role may be more complex (see Chapter 3, Section 3.8).

Following on from the 'approval for delivery' status of the apprenticeship, there is additional work to be negotiated and carried out. In setting up a higher- or degree-level apprenticeship in your organisation there are some common elements outlined in Figure 1a. There may be other considerations, such as how the provider, mentor and apprentice are collecting evidence to meet the apprenticeship standard – some providers are using technologies like SmartAssessor (there is more on this in Chapter 5). There may be subcontracting arrangements where providers share parts of the 'off-the-job' learning.

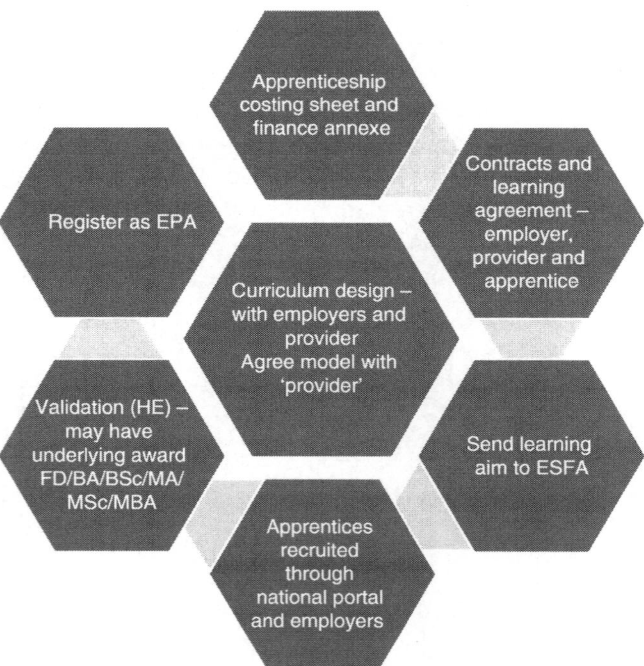


Figure 1a Setting up a higher- or degree-level apprenticeship

### *Activity 10*

- Looking back to the beginning of this chapter – can you situate your apprenticeship standard and your apprentices' learning experiences in relation to Aristotle's five ways of knowing:
  - technique (techné)
  - science (episteme)
  - practical sense (phronesis)
  - wisdom (sophia)
  - intelligence (nous)?
- What strengths, weaknesses, opportunities and threats are there for:

  a) higher- and degree-level apprentices and

  b) apprenticeship routes?

## 1.5 YOUR ACTION PLAN 1

### *Activity 11*

- Complete the action plan below based on the activities in this chapter. The table is available electronically at www.criticalpublishing.com/the-new-apprenticeships.

*Table 1d Your action plan 1*

| **Issue** | **Proposed actions** | **Responsibility for actions** | **Intended targets/ outcomes** | **Timing** |
|---|---|---|---|---|
| **1.1 Apprenticeships and trends in vocational education and training** | Eg, review the elements of my approach to vocational education and training | Myself and mentee | Broaden strategies I need to use if necessary | Immediate |
| **1.2 Vocational standards, qualifications and qualification frameworks: T levels and the future** | Eg, familiarise myself with any mandated qualifications in my apprentice's standard | Myself, training partners | Ensure work-based mentoring is related to mandated qualification | Next six months |

*(continued)*

| Issue | Proposed actions | Responsibility for actions | Intended targets/ outcomes | Timing |
|---|---|---|---|---|
| **1.3 The role of the trailblazers: the standards and the assessment plan** | Eg, familiarise myself with standard and assessment plan for apprenticeship | Myself | Modify work-placed mentoring in light of standard and assessment plan | Next six months |
| **1.4 Higher and degree apprenticeships** | Eg, find out about higher and degree apprenticeships in my vocational sector and geographical area | Myself | Engage with relevant local HEI departments | Immediate |

# 2 Learning and development

**CHAPTER CONTENT**

This chapter covers:



## 2.1 FEATURES OF VOCATIONAL LEARNERS AND LEARNING

The New Apprenticeships include the widest range of vocational learners of any previous vocational education programme. As seen in Chapter 1, they can be young people or adults, working at entry level/level 1, level 3, degree level or even at Master's/doctoral level. They may have little or considerable educational or work experience. They may have little or great life experience. They may previously have been successful or unsuccessful learners. However, whatever the features that may divide them, there are a number of important factors they will share.

- As apprentices, they are new to the *occupational roles* their apprenticeships will be preparing them for and therefore new to the knowledge, skills and attitudes they will eventually need to demonstrate.
- Their end-point assessment will have been designed using similar principles and quality assessed with the same rigour.
- They will be employed and therefore subject to the rules, regulations, expectations and cultures of their employers.

- Their learning mentors/coaches will be primarily concerned with their ability to demonstrate knowledge, skills and attitudes acquired on the job via experiential learning and reflection.

Ingle and Duckworth (2013) refer to the report of the Commission on Adult Vocational Teaching and Learning (CAVTL, 2013) in describing eight distinctive features of adult vocational teaching and learning.

1. *That through the combination of sustained practice and the understanding of theory, occupational expertise is developed.*
2. *That work-related attributes are central to the development of occupational expertise.*
3. *That practical problem-solving and critical reflection on experience, including learning from mistakes in real and simulated settings, are central to effective teaching and learning.*
4. *That vocational teaching and learning is most effective when it is collaborative and contextualised, taking place within communities of practice which involve different types of 'teacher' and capitalise on the experience and knowledge of all learners.*
5. *That technology plays a key role because keeping on top of technological advances is an essential part of the occupational expertise required in any workplace.*
6. *That it requires a range of assessment and feedback methods that involve both 'teachers' and learners, and which reflect the specific assessment cultures of different occupations and sectors.*
7. *That it often benefits from operating across more than one setting, including a real or simulated workplace, as well as the classroom and workshop, to develop the capacity to learn and apply that learning in different settings, just as at work.*
8. *That occupational standards are dynamic, evolving to reflect advances in work practices, and that through collective learning, transformation in quality and efficiency is achieved.*

## *Activity 1*

- Which of the eight features of vocational learning and teaching above are relevant to the learning of your apprentice?
- Rank them in order according to their importance to you.
- Ask your apprentice to rank them in order according to their importance to them.
- Was there any agreement between the two lists?

## Barriers to learning

Depending on their own biography so far, your apprentice is likely to have experienced barriers to their learning and may be anticipating having to overcome similar or further barriers to their learning in the course of their apprenticeship. One of your key roles is in helping them overcome these and the first stage is to ascertain which of these barriers might stand in the way of the successful completion of their apprenticeship. This will enable you to work on how to overcome such barriers and thereby identify the key learning needs your apprentice has.

### Barriers at work

For many young people beginning work, the environment offers many challenges that may affect their capacity to learn. They may find themselves isolated in a way they weren't with their mates at school or with fellow students on their college courses. They may find that shift work is requiring changed sleeping patterns and affecting their concentration. They may be subjected to discrimination or treatment by colleagues or supervisors who do not value them or their role. Their adjustment to full-time work may stand in the way of sustained concentrated study. Even the time and effort of travelling to and from work could affect their learning capacity.

### Socio-economic barriers

We know that factors such as poverty and family background are key factors affecting achievement in schools and colleges but these may well continue to affect an apprentice's current learning and achievement. We also know that peer pressure is a key influence on the achievement of adolescent and post-adolescent young people and that, again, this could affect an individual's vocational learning. Although we have rapidly become a digital society (89 per cent of adults in Great Britain used the internet at least weekly in 2018, up from 88 per cent in 2017 and 51 per cent in 2006; 46 per cent of adults watched videos on demand from commercial services in 2018, up from 29 per cent in 2016; the proportion of adults aged 65 years and over who shop online has trebled since 2008, rising from 16 per cent to 48 per cent in 2018 (Office for National Statistics, 2018)), there is still variation in access to the internet, often most limited in economically deprived households.

### Personal barriers

Related to socio-economic barriers are the many personal barriers that can affect learning. Apprentices may have or share caring roles that could involve childcare responsibilities. They may themselves have special educational needs or disabilities, often only recently confirmed. They may have acquired English as an additional language, which may make them slower to grasp the language of a specific occupational role.

### Emotional barriers

These can be the most formidable barriers to learning for apprentices to overcome. How does the maths-phobic on their second GCSE retake cope with the maths requirements of the occupational role? Many young adults starting work do so after many years of failure within a system that prizes academic achievement, leaving them with low levels of self-esteem and confidence. The vocational context can often provide the opportunities for such young people to start again, to see the relevance of their learning and to thrive and achieve.

### *Activity 2*

Below is the biographical profile of Michaela, a 25 year-old electrician who works for construction company Dunphy and Co.

- What, in your view, was a key barrier to learning she managed to overcome and what key need did she bring to her learning?

## Scenario

### Michaela

Staff at Michaela's primary school saw a very bright future for her: she did extremely well in her SATs and was expected to gain a place at grammar school in this selective borough. Nevertheless, she narrowly failed to get a place and found herself at the local high school. In Years 7 and 8, the achievement that marked her primary years continued, but things seemed to go wrong for her from Year 9 onwards. She began to bunk off school with a small group of friends she had fallen in with. Her parents were called into school on a number of occasions as a result of Michaela's poor behaviour. Both the school and her parents thought this change might be a result of post-adolescent rebellion but this behaviour continued into Years 10 and 11. Michaela seemed to have no interest in her GCSE courses and when the exams came, managed to turn up for only two or three. She scraped Cs in IT and physical education and sport. She spent three months in the sixth form on GCSE retakes but seemed even less motivated than she was first time round. Largely thanks to her uncle, who worked for the construction company Dunphy and Co, she was taken on as an apprentice electrician and enrolled at college part-time to take the level 2 diploma. Although conscientious at work, with good time-keeping and attendance, she seemed to be going through the motions, without enthusiasm and without any apparent ambition. Although she claimed to be doing well on her college course, college tutors got in touch with her employers on several occasions wondering where she was on college days. Michaela's employers gave her a final warning. Her college attendance improved but college reports on her progress confirmed that she was jumping through the hoops required and she managed to just about pass her level 2 diploma. Everything seemed to change when Michaela enrolled for level 3. At work, she began to put her own stamp on jobs and her co-workers were surprised at her capacity to solve problems in novel ways. She began to mention Tim Myers, her level 3 tutor. He had had his own successful electrician contractor business but had decided to retire early and retrain as a college teacher. Tim was familiar with all the latest developments in the field and his approach was workshop-based in which he used the working contexts of his students in a problem-solving approach. Michaela sailed through her level 3 and now has several years of varied experience with Dunphy. Her co-workers and her employers have recognised her potential as a leader, manager and supervisor and are prepared to sponsor her to attend construction site management courses.

A critical incident for Michaela seemed to occur at the beginning of her level 3 diploma course. Tim Myers suddenly takes prominence and it may be that, for the first time in her life, Michaela was able to see a connection between her learning at college and her performance at work; in other words, learning was *relevant* to her. Tim Myers' problem-solving approach was highly practical in nature and focused on the workplace. The recency of Tim Myer's experience probably gave him credibility and his history running a successful contracting company was a possible source of Michaela's new-found ambition. So the learning need that was met rather late in Michaela's learning career was the need for connections to be made between her learning on the one hand and her life and experience on the other. These connections had been missing from her school days from Year 9 onwards and from her early years of college and employment.

### *Activity 3*

- Create a biographical profile for your apprentice in similar detail and make a judgement about any learning need(s) they may be bringing to their apprenticeship.
- Ask them to create an autobiographical profile. Compare biography with autobiography.

## 2.2 FACTORS AFFECTING VOCATIONAL LEARNING

### Motivation

The most well-known theory of motivation is arguably Maslow's hierarchy of needs (Maslow, 1987).

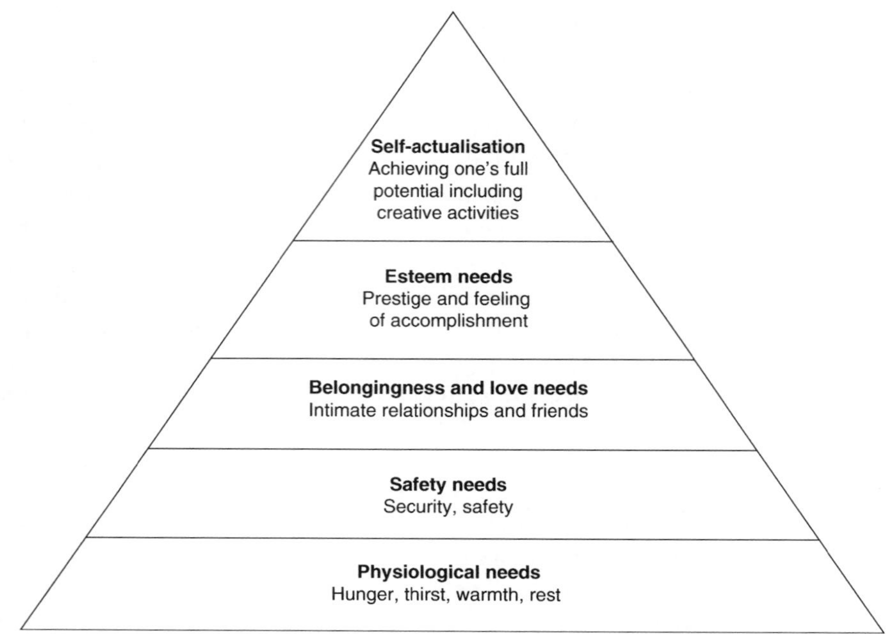


Figure 2a Maslow's hierarchy of needs

Maslow presents human needs in a hierarchical pyramid with basic, physiological needs such as hunger and thirst at the bottom. Once these needs are met, the next level contains psychological needs such as safety and security. A further level comprises social needs such as friendship and belonging, followed by the need for self-esteem and worth. The final level is self-actualisation, the desire to fulfil one's potential. Moving from one level to the next requires that the needs from the previous level have been met. And, for Maslow, it is the need for self-actualisation that drives people to learn. While learning may not always progress up a hierarchy as Maslow describes, the importance of wellbeing and self-esteem to effective learning for post-16 learners, particularly those in higher education, are key issues in current debates about education.

## Activity 4

- Consider each of the levels of needs in Maslow's hierarchy. To what extent are these important factors for your apprentice's learning at work and what implications do they have for your mentoring/coaching role?

The motive to learn in Maslow's hierarchy is to achieve self-actualisation, to engage in activities as ends in themselves, for one's own self-fulfilment. Such activity could be described as intrinsically motivated. However, we saw in Chapter 1 that one of the key aspects of vocational learning was that, traditionally, it has been associated with an extrinsic purpose, such as the preparation for work, as opposed to general education's more intrinsic purpose as an end in itself. And, indeed, those who undertake training and take vocational qualifications could be seen as extrinsically motivated to get on in their careers, to enjoy promotion and achieve higher status and pay levels. However, this is an over-simplification. How many of those seeking academic success at A level in order to progress to university will be doing it because of their intrinsic desire to learn rather than achieve higher status and enhance career opportunities? Michaela's eventual success at college and subsequent success at work above came about after her insight that her learning was connected with her capacity to do a good job, a kind of vocational self-actualisation, intrinsically motivated.

### *Activity 5*

- What does your apprentice think their motivation was to gain an apprenticeship? Were they intrinsically or extrinsically motivated?

## Ability

The practice of intelligence testing is still widespread and influential. It is the basis for selection for grammar schools in local authorities that still operate selective education and is used in different guises by some employers, including the civil service and armed forces, although the use of testing a wider range of abilities by employers is now common. Nevertheless, there is still no agreement on what 'intelligence' is and what its influence – together with other supposedly innate, inherited factors – on achievement actually is, as opposed to factors that are social and environmental, such as schooling and background.

For the purposes of vocational education, it might be more helpful to turn to those theorists who regard traditional academic achievement as reliant on a narrow range of ability but recognise that there is a range of other 'intelligences' that might be valuable in the workplace. For Howard Gardner, an intelligence:

> *entails the ability to solve problems or fashion products that are of consequence in a particular cultural setting or community. The problem-solving skill allows one to approach a situation in which a goal is to be obtained and to locate the appropriate route to that goal. The creation of a cultural product allows one to capture and transmit knowledge or to express one's conclusions, beliefs, or feelings. The problems to be solved range from creating an end for a story to anticipating a mating move in chess to repairing a quilt. Products range from scientific theories to musical compositions to successful political campaigns.*
>
> (Gardner, 2006, p 8)

Gardner proposes six different kinds of intelligent behaviour. As well as that which underpins academic achievement, logical-mathematical intelligence, there are, according to Gardner, linguistic, spatial, musical, bodily kinaesthetic and personal intelligences (interpersonal intelligence or the capacity to relate to others and intrapersonal intelligence or emotional self-awareness).

These latter two are close to what Daniel Goleman (1998) has described as 'emotional intelligence'. He identified five social and emotional competencies.

1. Self-awareness – understand one's emotions, strengths and weaknesses, and recognise their impact on others.
2. Self-regulation – manage one's feelings and adapt to changing circumstances.
3. Social skills – manage others' feelings well.
4. Empathy – recognise, understand, and consider other people's feelings.
5. Motivation – using your feelings to achieve your goals.

### *Activity 6*

Return to Activity 6 in Chapter 1. This asked you to identify knowledge and skills and qualities you would deem essential to be included in the standard for your apprentice. Then, on the Institute for Apprenticeship's website www.instituteforapprenticeships.org/apprenticeship-standards you were asked to locate the approved standard that is the closest to your apprenticeship and estimate how far the items of knowledge, skills and qualities you identified were reflected in that standard.

- What implications does this have for your approach to mentoring and coaching your apprentice?

## Age and development

The notion that the capacity to learn was fixed on reaching adulthood and then gradually diminished as one aged has been largely discredited and it is now accepted that adulthood is a period of change and development and that the capacity to learn is not significantly reduced. This is reflected in the design of the New Apprenticeships, which are not just for school leavers and young people; there is no upper age limit and anyone over 16, living in England and not in full-time education is eligible to become an apprentice. So an apprenticeship could be for someone moving into their first job, someone promoted into a new role that requires them to take on new responsibilities and exercise new skills and abilities, or someone changing career.

You may, however, be mentoring an apprentice who is in the period of late or post-adolescence (16+) and therefore subject to some of the changes that may influence their learning. According to Armitage et al:

*Adolescent development can be divided into three broad areas:*

- *Physical*
  - *rapid weight and height growth*
  - *puberty – development of hormones and secondary sex characteristics (eg, facial hair in males)*
  - *brain development – particularly that affecting emotional, physical and mental proficiency*
- *Cognitive: development of*
  - *reasoning*
  - *abstract thinking (the ability to interpret images and ideas in a different way from that which is merely presented literally). Abstract thinking is normally contrasted with concrete thinking in which an individual is able to is able to ascribe literal meaning to only to an object or idea*
  - *meta-cognition (the ability to think about thinking)*
- *Psycho-social*
  - *establishing an identity – including that of sexuality*
  - *working towards and gaining independence*
  - *the ability to develop close relationships and intimacy.*

(Armitage et al, 2011, p 58)

### *Activity 7*

- If your apprentice is at the late or post-adolescent stage, is there any aspect of their development that has had an impact on their vocational learning?

## Andragogy and pedagogy

Malcolm Knowles made the distinction between andragogy, '*the art and science of helping adults learn*', and pedagogy, '*the art and science of teaching children*' (Knowles et al, 2015, p 61). This distinction has five features or assumptions as outlined in Table 2a.

*Table 2a The assumptions of andragogy*

| | Pedagogical | Andragogical |
|---|---|---|
| **Concept of the learner** | Dependent personality | Increasingly self-directed |
| **Role of learner's experience** | To be built on | A rich resource for learning by self and others |
| **Readiness to learn** | Uniform by age, level and curriculum | Develops from life tasks and problems |
| **Orientation to learning** | Subject-centred | Task- or problem-centred |
| **Motivation** | By external rewards and punishment | By internal incentives and curiosity |

Adapted from Knowles et al, 2015

So, for Knowles, while the child is dependent on the teacher or other adult to guide them in their learning, the adult learner is more reliant on themselves to take charge of their learning. Equally, the child comes to learning with limited previous learning and experience of the world, while the adult has a fund of previous learning and life experience to fall back on. A child's readiness to learn is determined by their age, the level at which they are learning and the stage in the curriculum they have reached, while the adult's readiness to learn will have much to do with the stage of their lives and their motivation for learning. While a child is accustomed to learning in specific subjects, the adult will see learning as a set of tasks or problems to be solved. And, for Knowles, while children are extrinsically motivated, adults are intrinsically motivated.

There are those who question Knowles' first assumption, pointing to the many children who seem self-directed in their learning and perfectly happy to work without an adult's guidance. They also point out that many adults, in particular those returning to learn for the first time since school, can have a high dependency on tutors and other adults ('*Just show me what to do and how to do it!*'). Knowles' second assumption, that adults have a rich reservoir of experience, suggests that experiential learning is always going to be the right approach for them while other approaches to learning, the absorption and processing of information, for example, might well be appropriate at times. And many psychologists point out that the experiences of a child's early years, particularly the first five, could be important influences on their subsequent learning and development. Knowles' third assumption, that children's readiness to learn is connected to their age, level and the curriculum, is something of a self-fulfilling prophecy, since they are subjected to such structures as a result of the principles of educational psychology and policy. And many adults, university students as well as those taking vocational qualifications, for example, are highly aware of the level at which they are working and the requirements of the curriculum they are following. Knowles' claim that children's orientation is subject-oriented would be questioned by anyone walking into a primary classroom and asking the children what the subject they were studying was, particularly if they were following an integrated curriculum. And, with regard to motivation, many children, particularly those in primary classrooms, learn happily much of the time without the promise of reward or the threat of punishment.

## *Activity 8*

- Are there any features of pedagogy or andragogy that can be accurately applied to your learning as a child or adult or to that of your apprentice?
- If andragogy accurately described adult learning, what implications would there be for your apprentice's learning?

## 2.3 COMMUNICATION AND INTERACTION

There are two dimensions of communication and interaction that should concern the mentor/coach of an apprentice. The first relates to communication *between* the mentor/coach and their apprentice; the second is connected with the apprentice's own communication as part of their occupational role.

### Transactional analysis

In relation to the first, many find transactional analysis a useful tool to examine interactions. Transactional analysis (TA) was first popularised by Eric Berne in the 1960s (Berne, 1961, 1964). It's a '*tool that... can be used as a teaching or learning device for understanding behaviour in human interaction*' (Quinn, 2000). Berne describes transactional analysis as a system of feelings accompanied by a relative set of behaviour patterns. These are what Berne calls three '*ego states*': '*parent*', which is based on transactions that took place in the formative years – the internalised parental 'dos' and 'don'ts'; '*child*', based on internal events, positive and negative feelings and responses from the first five years; and '*adult*', exerting control over the world, examining both the parent and the child data against the reality of today, accepting it or rejecting it as appropriate, and estimating probability in order to devise solutions. Each interaction between two people with one of these ego states is deemed a '*transaction*'. Berne's first rule of communications concerns crossed transactions: as long as transactions remain complementary there is nothing to break the stimulus–response process and the exchange can continue indefinitely (see Figure 2b).

> *The unit of social intercourse is called a transaction. If two or more people encounter each other... sooner or later one of them will speak, or give some other indication of acknowledging the presence of the others. This is called transactional stimulus. Another person will then say or do something which is in some way related to the stimulus, and that is called the transactional response.*
>
> (Berne, 1964)

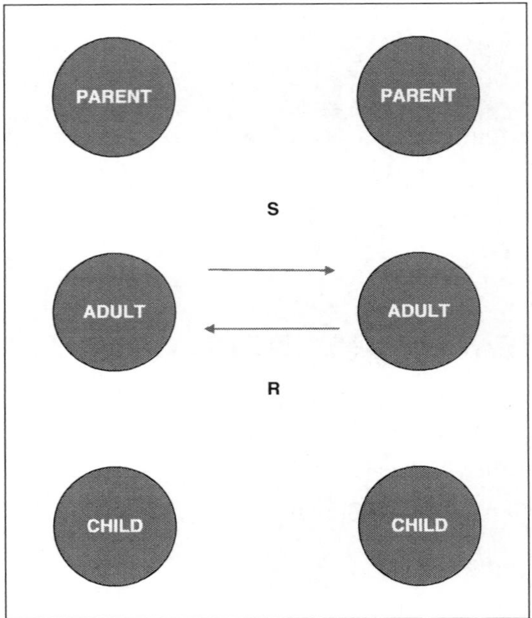


Figure 2b An adult–adult complementary transaction

Berne's second rule of communication concerns crossed transactions (see Figure 2c): when a transaction is crossed, a break in communications occurs and one or both individuals will need to change ego states in order for communication to be re-established. Here, the adult stimulus is adult to adult. However, the response is like that of a child to a parent.

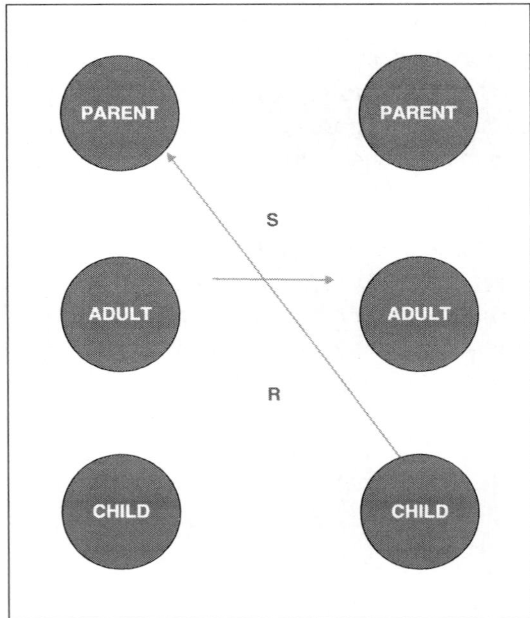


Figure 2c Crossed transaction

Berne's third rule of communication concerns ulterior transactions. In ulterior transactions, two messages are conveyed simultaneously: one is an overt, social level message, the other a covert, psychological message. The behavioural outcome of an ulterior transaction is determined at the psychological not the social level. An example he gives is expressed diagrammatically in Figure 2d.

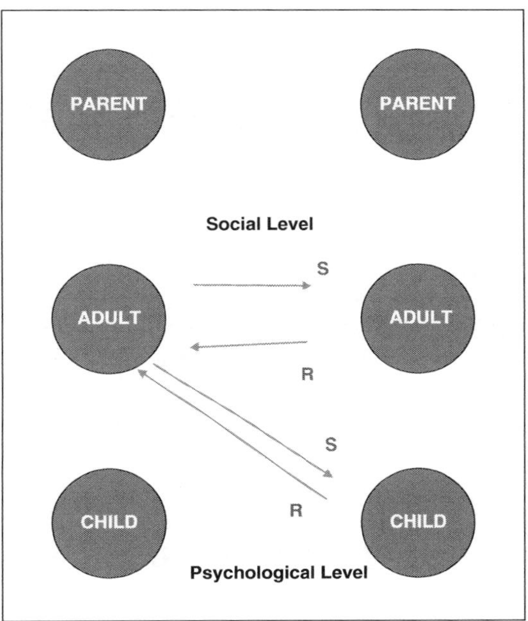


Figure 2d An adult angular ulterior transaction

Berne describes the transaction in Figure 2d as follows:

> *Salesman: This one is better, but you can't afford it. Customer: That's the one I'll take. The salesman, as Adult, states two objective facts: 'This one is better' and 'You can't afford it'. At the ostensible, or social, level these are directed to the Adult of the customer, whose Adult reply would be: 'You are correct on both counts.' However, the ulterior, or psychological, vector is directed by the well trained and experienced Adult of the salesman to the customer's Child. The correctness of his judgement is demonstrated by the Child's reply, which says in effect: 'Regardless of the financial consequences, I'll show that arrogant fellow I'm as good as any of his customers.' At both levels the transactions are complementary, since the customer's reply is accepted at face value as an Adult purchasing contract.*
>
> (Berne, 1964, p 31)

## *Activity 9*

An example of a crossed transaction at work might be as follows.

**Supervisor:** (Grabbing measure) *Look – I thought I told you to allow for the thickness of the wood strip! Let me show you again.* (Parent to child)

**Apprentice:** *You never let me try to do things myself, do you?* (Child to parent)

**Supervisor:** *OK, I'm sorry.* (Handing measure back) *Have another try.* (Changes ego state from parent to adult)

**Apprentice:** *Right, thanks*. (Changes ego state from child to adult)

- Can you think of any crossed or ulterior transactions you have had with your apprentice?
- Berne says '*when a transaction is crossed, a break in communications occurs and one or both individuals will need to change ego states in order for communication to be re-established*'. How did you change ego states in order for communication to continue?

# Communication relating to an occupational role

Any occupational role will have a range of communication requirements in relation to which the apprentice will need to develop proficiency. These may be requirements for spoken communication – giving commands, asking questions and eliciting information, conducting phone conversations – or for written communication – writing reports, completing forms, conveying information, sending emails.

## *Activity 10*

- In the left-hand column of Table 2b are a number of examples of the oral and written communication requirements of occupational roles. Add to these any that you and your apprentice think are relevant to their specific occupational role. Referring to the behaviours, skills and knowledge of the standards and the assessment plan of their occupational role might help you with this.
- Once you have completed the left-hand column, both of you should decide on a proficiency rating for the apprentice for each relevant requirement, where 10 is high, 1 is low, and record it in the second column.
- Take all those that scored 5 or below and, in the third column, suggest how the apprentice's proficiency might be improved. The table is available at www.criticalpublishing.com/the-new-apprenticeships should you wish to complete it electronically.

*Table 2b Activity 10*

| Communication requirement | Proficiency rating | How might proficiency be improved? |
|---|---|---|
| 1. Clarity of/articulation in spoken expression | 3 | For example:<br>• record and listen to conversations<br>• ask others for feedback on recorded conversations<br>• seek feedback – colleagues, tutors, mentor<br>• phone conversations – seek feedback on clarity<br>• seek practice or advice in functional skills/GCSE sessions |
| 2. Audible volume in spoken expression | | |
| 3. Giving clear instructions | | |
| 4. Following instructions | | |
| 5. Relating events in a clear, logical narrative | | |
| 6. Expressing a point of view | | |
| 7. Resolving conflicts and misunderstandings | | |
| 8. Chairing or contributing to a meeting | | |
| 9. Conducting a phone conversation effectively | | |
| 10. Persuading | | |
| 11. Negotiating | | |
| 12. Writing a report | | |
| 13. Drawing up an agreement | | |
| 14. Writing emails that are clear and unambiguous | | |
| 15. Recording events in a clear, logical narrative | | |
| 16. Taking accurate and full minutes | | |
| 17. Designing an event programme | | |
| 18. Creating a poster | | |
| 19. Writing a business letter | | |
| 20. Others? | | |

## 2.4 LEARNING THEORIES

Although learning theorists offer their own views on how the most effective learning takes place, a consideration of each of their theories can give apprentices and their mentors, coaches and trainers valuable insights into apprentice learning.

## Behaviourism

The essence of behaviourism is that learning involves changes in observable behaviour; not that learning *brings about* those changes but that the behavioural changes can be measured and comprise the learning itself. Many will be familiar with Pavlov's dogs. While measuring the salivation rates of dogs, Pavlov, a Russian physiologist, found that they would produce saliva when they heard or smelt food in anticipation of feeding. This is a normal reflex response which would be expected to happen, as saliva plays a role in the digestion of food. However, the dogs also began to salivate when events occurred that would otherwise be unrelated to feeding, such as the opening of a door by their feeder. This response demonstrated the basic principle of 'classical conditioning' or the association of a neutral stimulus (a door opening) with an unconditioned stimulus (being fed). B F Skinner's (1938) experiments with rats established 'operant conditioning', so called because the experimental rats had to act on the environment or operate a lever to obtain food. Behaviourists believe that learning proceeds step by step and builds on previously learnt behaviour. And the key person here is the teacher or learning facilitator, because they are the ones who manipulate the stimulus and manage the response in learning. Perhaps because early work to establish behaviourism was carried out with animals and also because systems of rewards and punishments, or positive or negative re-enforcers, are most familiar in primary classrooms (with gold stars accumulating against names on a wall chart), behaviourism is often thought to be a crude or rudimentary learning theory; but it has been hugely influential within education and across our lives. We saw in Chapter 1 how learning was assessed in NVQs, the most widely used vocational qualifications of the past 30 years, by measuring competencies that met performance criteria but also demonstrated underpinning knowledge and values, all through observable behaviour. And consider the role of behaviourism in psychotherapeutic approaches such as cognitive behavioural therapy, or dieting systems, for example.

## Cognitivist/constructivist approaches

We saw in Chapter 1 that while some commentators were happy with the competence based approach to learning of NVQ for more obviously skill-based learning, it was argued that its application was considered inappropriate to professional contexts that require greater knowledge and understanding, such as nurse education, social work training, teacher education or police training. This is because behaviourism ignores the role of cognition in learning, which is highly prized by those who subscribe to cognitivist or constructivist theories of learning. Gestalt theory – 'Gestalt' means form or shape in German – describes how we discern patterns or shapes in what we perceive and how we use closure to create a sum or whole out of constituent parts. Gestalt theory describes how we may achieve insights, or 'Eureka moments', when we suddenly 'get it'.

Piaget claimed that learning was developmental, and he identified stages in the intellectual development of children (Boden, 1994). These stages are the sensory-motor (0–2 years), when the child is learning through walking, talking and playing and developing a sense of self; the pre-operational, before the child is able to form concepts or abstract ideas (2–6 years); the concrete operational, when the child's mind is focused on the material world in front of it (7–11 years); and the formal operational (11+ years), at which point the child is capable of complex reasoning away from the material world, such as creating and testing hypotheses.

Bruner (1960) championed discovery learning which, for him, was the most effective way of understanding the principles of a subject. Through a problem-solving approach, learners are able to construct their own knowledge for themselves. The role of the teacher is to organise and facilitate the most effective way to do this and Bruner explained how this was possible through the concept of the spiral curriculum. This involved information being structured so that ideas can be taught at a simple level first and then at more complex levels later on.

## Social learning theories

It is claimed that '*social learning theories may be seen as a sort of bridge between behaviourism and cognitive theories of learning*' (Armitage et al, 2016, p 81). Vygotsky (1978) stressed the effect of the social factors in learning, particularly social interaction. He emphasised the communication between the learner and what he called the '*more knowledgeable other*' in moving from an existing level of knowledge to developing new knowledge. The gap between these two states was called the Zone of Proximal Development and effective learning comprised the navigation across this zone with the learner using the more knowledgeable other and facilitative techniques such as scaffolding to support this journey.

Bandura (1977) believed the most effective form of learning was through modelling or by the learner's intelligent imitation.

> *What are the characteristics of effective models? We do not automatically copy others and would need to be motivated to do so. Models are most effective when they (i) show confidence, (ii) are perceived by the observer to have similarities between himself/herself and the model, (iii) have credibility, ie models who practise what they preach and (iv) show enthusiasm – models who glow with interest in what they are doing or saying are more likely to influence observers.*
>
> (Child, 1997, p 163)

You might be reminded here of the 'Sitting-next-to-Nellie' approach, the most common form of training generally associated with apprenticeships and mentioned in Chapter 3, Section 3.3 about the mentoring cycle.

## Humanist theories

Knowles' theory of andragogy, described above, puts him squarely in the humanist tradition of learning theorists. Humanist theorists, notably Carl Rogers (1994), believe the key to effective learning is the activity of the learners themselves. Rogers has a counselling/psychotherapy background and it is therefore no surprise that his approach to learning is one of personal growth and development. For the humanist, the important person for the learner is not a teacher but a learning facilitator who can help the learner along the journey of growth and development. Because of the importance of the whole person in learning, the quality of the relationship of learner and facilitator is key in this process and the humanist would stress the importance of 'learning by doing' or experiential learning. Maslow, with his hierarchy of needs, falls within the humanist tradition and Rogers would have agreed with Maslow that self-actualisation was the ultimate goal of education and development.

### *Activity 11*

- Are any of the insights of the learning theories described above helpful in understanding your apprentice's learning?

## 2.5 LEARNING STYLES

The idea that we each have a preferred learning style is very attractive: identify the learning style and the mentor or coach can then create the optimum learning strategies, learning environment and resource for each learner. However, some commentators have raised questions about learning style models: Coffield and colleagues (2004) examined 13 out of 71 models and found only three passed their test for consistency, reliability and validity. Furthermore, there are potential dangers in identifying types of learner, principally the danger of stereotyping individuals and the over-simplistic assumption that any one learner learns in a specific kind of way. Nevertheless, there is a consensus among many experienced teachers and learners that individuals may use one or more of a number of preferred learning styles in the course of their learning career.

- Those preferring a visual style respond well to visual stimuli, whether they be PowerPoint demonstrations or video clips. Visual learners need to see things in pictures not words. They have high spatial intelligence and a keen sense of design, and find it easy to relate objects to one another on a visual plane.
- With an auditory style, learners respond well to auditory stimuli – to podcasts, songs and music. They make keen and intelligent listeners to lectures and talks.
- Those preferring a kinaesthetic style are sensitive to touch and movement. They might want to have a physical representation of an abstract idea and respond well to stimuli from the physical environment.
- Verbal learning requires sensitivity to the medium of language, whether it be in written or spoken form, and a desire to hear or read what is learned rather than see or feel it. Those who learn verbally often make good linguists.
- Logical/mathematical learning is rational thinking that seeks to understand the underpinning principles of arguments and systems. Material is absorbed most effectively when it is logically ordered and presented. Learners will want to sort disorganised material into their own logical categories.

- Intrapersonal learning is most effective when learners are alone rather than with others in social groups. They often say they need to go off and work something out for themselves. They need to take ownership of material and organise it into their own personal categories.
- Interpersonal learning happens best in social groups. Such learning requires sensitivity to others and the capacity to interpret visual cues and communication by others.

Chapter 3 considers Kolb's (1984) conception of the process of experiential learning as the basis for a mentoring cycle. His learning style model followed this and was the inspiration for Honey and Mumford's (1982) identification of four learning styles.

***Activists:*** *activists involve themselves fully and without bias in new experiences. They enjoy the here and now, and are happy to be dominated by immediate experiences. They are open-minded, not sceptical, and this tends to make them enthusiastic about anything new. Their philosophy is: 'I'll try anything once'. They tend to act first and consider the consequences afterwards.*

***Theorists:*** *theorists adapt and integrate observations into complex but logically sound theories. They think problems through in a vertical, step-by-step, logical way. They assimilate disparate facts into coherent theories. They tend to be perfectionists who won't rest easy until things are tidy and fit into a rational scheme. They like to analyse and synthesize.*

***Pragmatists:*** *pragmatists are keen on trying out ideas, theories and techniques to see if they work in practice. They positively search out new ideas and take the first opportunity to experiment with applications. They are the sort of people who return from courses brimming with new ideas that they want to try out in practice. They like to get on with things and act quickly and confidently on ideas that attract them.*

***Reflectors:*** *reflectors like to stand back to ponder experiences and observe them from many different perspectives. They collect data, both first hand and from others, and prefer to think about it thoroughly before coming to a conclusion. The thorough collection and analysis of data about experiences and events is what counts so they tend to postpone reaching definitive conclusions for as long as possible. Their philosophy is to be cautious. They are thoughtful people who like to consider all possible angles and implications before making a move.*

## Activity 12

- Does your apprentice have any preferred learning styles relating to their learning on the apprenticeship programme?

## 2.6 DEEP AND SURFACE LEARNING

Marton and Säljö (1976) first developed the notions of deep and surface learning through research they carried out with Swedish university students. They discovered that one group of students had focused on the facts and basic information in a text, while another had tried to understand the key arguments and rationale underpinning the text. These two approaches they deemed surface and deep learning.

Table 2c, adapted from Houghton (2004), compares the characteristics and factors that encourage deep and surface approaches to learning by university engineering students and their teachers. Compiled from Biggs (1999), Entwistle (1988) and Ramsden (1992).

*Table 2c Deep and surface learning*

| | **Deep learning** | **Surface learning** |
|---|---|---|
| **Definition** | • Examining new facts and ideas critically, and tying them into existing cognitive structures and making numerous links between ideas | • Accepting new facts and ideas uncritically and attempting to store them as isolated, unconnected items |
| **Characteristics** | • Looking for meaning | • Relying on rote learning |
| | • Focusing on the central argument or concepts needed to solve a problem | • Focusing on outwards signs and the formulae needed to solve a problem |
| | • Interacting actively | • Receiving information passively |
| | • Distinguishing between argument and evidence | • Failing to distinguish principles from examples |
| | • Making connections between different modules | • Treating parts of modules and programmes as separate |
| | • Relating new and previous knowledge | • Not recognising new material as building on previous work |
| | • Linking course content to real life | • Seeing course content simply as material to be learnt for the exam |
| **Encouraged by students** | • Being intrinsically curious about the subject | • Studying a degree for the qualification and not being interested in the subject |
| | • Being determined to do well and mentally engaging when doing academic work | • Not focusing on academic areas, but emphasising others (eg, social, sport) |
| | • Having the appropriate background knowledge for a sound foundation | • Lacking background knowledge and understanding necessary to understand material |
| | • Having time to pursue interests, through good time management | • Not enough time/too high a workload |
| | • Positive experience of education leading to confidence in ability | • Cynical view of education, believing that factual recall is what is required |
| | • To understand and succeed | • High anxiety |

| | Deep learning | Surface learning |
|---|---|---|
| **Encouraged by teachers** | • Showing personal interest in the subject | • Conveying disinterest or even a negative attitude to the material |
| | • Bringing out the structure of the subject | • Presenting material so that it can be perceived as a series of unrelated facts and ideas |
| | • Concentrating on and ensuring plenty of time for key concepts | |
| | • Confronting students' misconceptions | |
| | • Engaging students in active learning | • Allowing students to be passive |
| | | • Assessing for independent facts (short-answer questions) |
| | • Using assessments that require thought, and require ideas to be used together | • Rushing to cover too much material and emphasising coverage at the expense of depth |
| | • Relating new material to what students already know and understand | |
| | • Allowing students to make mistakes without penalty and rewarding effort | • Creating undue anxiety or low expectations of success by discouraging statements or excessive workload |
| | • Being consistent and fair in assessing declared intended learning outcomes, and hence establishing trust | • Having a short assessment cycle |

Adapted from Houghton, 2004

### *Activity 13*

- Looking at the factors in Table 2c, how far do the approaches to learning you take with your apprentice encourage deep or surface learning?

## 2.7 LEARNING IN ORGANISATIONS

In his seminal *The Fifth Discipline*, Peter Senge (2006) described five features organisations need in order to describe themselves as 'learning organisations'. These were as follows.

1. **Systems thinking.** This focuses on the extent to which the organisation is aware of how the people, structures and processes, or the different parts of the organisation relate to one another best in order to make the organisation function well. It is also concerned with how far the organisation relates to the immediate and wider environments it works in.

2. **Personal mastery**. It is important for individuals to be open to learning, not just in the formal training the organisation may offer, but in their everyday working lives. Learning organisations have a culture of learning and regard their members' capacity to learn, both quickly and effectively, as key to the organisation's success.
3. **Mental models**. Mental models constitute the conceptual frameworks each of us possess and are the lenses through which we see, experience and understand the world. However, since these are fixed, this may lead to misinterpretation and miscommunication relating to facts and experiences that do not fit into our mental models. Similarly, an organisation may have overriding mental models regarding its norms, values and ways of operation. A learning organisation should have an open culture in which mental models can be challenged in order that individuals and the organisation can learn, adapt and change.
4. **Shared vision**. The individuals of a learning organisation should have a shared vision about the rationale, nature, purpose and direction of the organisation in order to maximise the effectiveness of their learning and development.
5. **Team learning**. Team learning can be learning *in* teams or sharing learning *across* teams. Learning organisations have systems and structures which facilitate this learning and maximise the knowledge and expertise of the workforce as a whole.

## *Activity 14*

- How far would you and your apprentice describe the organisation you work for as a 'learning organisation'?

## *Activity 15*

- In Chapter 3, Section 3.9, you are asked about maintaining your occupational currency and ensuring your continuous professional development. How many of the activities below would be available for this in your organisation?
  - Observations of your practice – by colleagues, managers, staff developers.
  - Appraisals.
  - Mentoring.
  - Involvement in subject/skills area network meetings.
  - Training in emerging technologies.
  - Conference attendance.

- Organisation staff development days.
- Action learning sets (a group of work-based colleagues who meet regularly – at each, one presents a work-related problem and the others, guided by a facilitator, discuss and analyse this problem).
- Recording experiences, meetings, professional activities, thoughts/ideas.
- Professional/occupational updating.
- Learning visit to industry/commercial organisation, public services.
- Secondment.
- Updating knowledge through TV, internet, social media.
- Short courses.
- Consultancy.
- Research projects.
- Gaining literacy, numeracy and English for speakers of other languages (ESOL) qualifications.
- Shadowing.
- Awarding organisation subject-specific updating.
- Taking on examiner, verifier or assessor responsibilities.
- Organising trips, residentials and work placements.

## 2.8 CURRENT AND EMERGING TECHNOLOGIES

## Virtual, augmented realities and simulation technologies

As a rule, authenticity in learning experiences is important, and the learning and skills sector has made a virtue of this over the years, with carpenters in workshops, chefs in kitchens and hairdressers in salons. But 'authentic' isn't always practicable, possible or safe. Two new technologies are augmented reality and virtual reality.

### Augmented reality

Students with mobile devices are able to tap into information based on the location they are in, where reality can be augmented, as well as the location where they would like to be, as in virtual reality. Augmented reality provides an overlay of information on a screen taken from a location where the viewer has pointed a device. Augmented reality requires the 'in the location' of a recognised place or co-ordinates to overlay information. Visiting a cathedral or art gallery is a good example of the value of augmented reality learning. By pointing a mobile device at a picture or artefact, information appears providing an explanation, or a video of the artist begins where the work being viewed is explained and discussed.

### Virtual reality

Virtual reality on the other hand is a totally created world that is viewed on mobile devices when the location of viewing is irrelevant. So in a virtual world, students explore real places using realistic 3D imaging. In these circumstances, virtual reality creates an immersive experience. Consider a geography class on the rock structures of Ayers Rock/ Uluru in Australia or visiting the surface of the Moon. Students can control the experience by wearing goggles that track head movements giving the effect of 'being there'. Learning comes to life.

### Simulation technology

Simulation technology replaces authentic learning of any kind where the 'authenticity' of learning is too expensive, too far away or presents health and safety issues. So a mechanic can use a computer to practise paint-spraying. An architect can design a building and then walk through it. Pilots, drivers, machine operators and crane drivers can all practise their basic skills without risk to life and property. Consider trying to teach a group how to use welding equipment. Immediately there is the cost of material and power and environmental issues, as well as the health and safety issues of using a welding gun for the first time. All illustrate the value of simulation technologies. In one FE college where virtual reality welding is done, art students have also used the equipment to practise the skills needed for making metal sculptures, at no extra cost to the college!

## Personal learning spaces

Personal learning spaces provide each apprentice with a space for learning that is cloud-based. They are often shortened to the term 'e-portfolio'. In effect e-portfolios are a lot more than a simple storage facility or indexing of relevant content. They are online places used to demonstrate learning. They come in two forms: mapping and reflective.

### Mapping portfolios

Mapping portfolios allow indexing but then allow space for adding a narrative as a means of bringing coherence to what has been captured. They tend to be front-loaded with a series of competencies or learning outcomes that the owner then maps experiences and achievements to in order to complete the programme. There are many mapping portfolio options available to use because the behaviour of an apprentice is easy to capture in the software for mapping portfolios. They are used extensively in NVQ programmes.

### Reflective portfolios

Reflective portfolios are harder to build. They tend to be 'open spaces', which invite the owner to create what might be called a learning contract and then populate it accordingly. Rather than mapping, the student adds a narrative of learning. Using personal learning spaces gives students new opportunities to capture their unique learning experiences and ideas when convenient in terms of place and time for them. It allows the capture of opportunistic learning (which can then be shared) and encourages students to take more responsibility for managing their own learning as a result, in any current period of learning, any previous learning that informed the choice, and in terms of what should follow on. If all this is captured on mobile personal devices and the information and order of learning is held in cloud spaces, then students and their growing body of evidence, work, accomplishments and achievements are never far away from each other and are available for sharing as required. Modern technology also makes much better use of videos and pictures, meaning evidence can be added to explanations and demonstrations of work, capturing competence 'in action' and not relying on a witness statement. This comes with the added authenticity of hearing the student explaining or seeing them showing their own learning rather than relying on written statements of others and adding photographed signatures.

## Social media

One aspect of distance learning or, at least, learning undertaken at distance, is the loss of a sense of a group of like-minded people, working together, supporting each other on the way to a common goal, in a way that includes sharing of useful resources, encouragement during difficult periods on the programme and a sense of shared excitement of achieving. The use of online messaging provides a ready source for socialisation in learning and the ability to share content. A message can include pictures and videos. Students are able to capture serendipitous and accidental learning moments with others immediately. Personal applications allow students to capture content that is uploaded later. Consequently, social media give an immediacy to learning and with it genuine socialisation. It can replace the fog of emails and copies of messages with one single 'in the moment' long conversation.

## Flip and blend

Learning technologies are particularly good at supporting cognitive domain learning but less good at learning in the affective domain. A health studies student can memorise and practise recall of aspects of the Mental Health Act but technology can't do such a good job at providing an authentic sense of what it might mean to be a social worker. Clearly teachers need to design the deployment of technology where it brings value to learning. Consequently, being able to recall information in class, where a teacher can help translate it into understanding, is a better way of working. The homework *precedes* the class and is knowledge preparation rather than knowledge rehearsal when homework is set to be done *after* a class. This is where learning is flipped. It allows the class time spent with a tutor to make the most of the experience and craft of the tutor. Why would we ask a chef to teach a recipe for a soufflé in the kitchen when the time is better spent making, touching, tasting and enjoying the art of cooking one under expert guidance? This mixing together of content in different formats, combining online with location learning, tutorial support and recorded mentor feedback is how learning is blended together, using people, devices, content repositories, time, places and the internet. Blended learning is not just a simple binary choice between a tutor and a computer, but a real mashing together of all of the above, so the lines all blur but still hold together and make sense due to the shared learning outcomes previously agreed and worked towards.

## The virtual class

Technology is equally valuable in running virtual classrooms. It can facilitate the meeting of a large class of students with tutors, experts, authors and others, including workplace mentors in virtual classes. Virtual classes support social cohesion as they offer opportunities to bring like-minded people together, but they have value in providing the opportunities to ask tutors questions. They allow a guest author or speaker to answer questions or talk to students without the need for travel, which is particularly useful if the author lives overseas. Virtual classes are great class maintenance opportunities, particularly for those who are absent from a class due to work, family commitments or illness. Virtual classes can be ad hoc arrangements as required or programmed into the study programme.

## Online learning objects

Learning resources are produced by tutors for their students, but learning objects tend to be more formed and structured and contain an introduction and at least some formative assessment. In every programme there are pockets of learning that are mainly factual in content and in need of being committed to memory. Mini online learning objects can be written then completed by students in a prescribed timeframe or tackled as part of a longer project. They run for each student and can provide pick-up points for continuing the learning. These mini learning objects can be added as a bank to one or more programmes (depending on the nature of the object) to be completed at some point in the programme as additional reading. They can relate to learning generally (a programme on Harvard referencing or study skills for example) or be very subject- or programme-specific. The repeatable nature of using learning objects in this way makes them ideal for reference or as using repetition to commit to memory to support more complex learning. They can free up time to do other things in the class (see 'Flip and blend', above).

## Apprenticeships

A feature of personal learning technologies is that they encourage better self-management of learning through controlling the learning and its direction and pace. It allows learning to be presented as being continuous, seamless and progressive, where each episode of learning helps define for the individual what comes next. What comes next can be added to what came before.

For apprentices, this is invaluable because these new portfolio technologies allow each student to capture, record, marshal, order, publish and present their learning and accomplishments. It can all be set against a learning agreement, which again can be as personalised as the learning required by the apprentice and the practice required by the employer. Consequently each apprentice can show a unique learning journey or at least a unique collection of evidence against a commonly agreed learning journey. Mentors, supporters, employers and other apprentices can collaborate and support the apprentice, creating a community of mutually supportive learning. Crucially, the apprentice can show what they have achieved with the support of others, rather than only be validated by others.

### *Activity 16*

- Consider the technology used in your apprentice's learning. Are there ways in which this could be used more effectively?

## 2.9 YOUR ACTION PLAN 2

### *Activity 17*

- Complete the action plan below based on the activities in this chapter. Table 2d is available electronically at www.criticalpublishing.com/the-new-apprenticeships.

*Table 2d Your action plan 2*

| Issue | Proposed actions | Responsibility for actions | Intended targets/ outcomes | Timing |
|---|---|---|---|---|
| **2.1 Features of vocational learners and learning** | Eg, establish apprentice's key learning needs | Coach and apprentice | Design learning that meets those needs | Immediate |
| **2.2 Factors affecting vocational learning** | Eg, identify how each key factor affects apprentice's vocational learning | Coach and apprentice | Design learning that takes those key factors into consideration | Immediate |
| **2.3 Communication and interaction** | Eg, identify key communication issues between you and apprentice and apprentice and colleagues | Coach and apprentice | Work to resolve any issues | Six months |
| **2.4 Learning theories** | Eg, identify elements in learning theories that could help apprentice learning | Coach and apprentice | Establish different kinds of learning in occupational role | Six months |
| **2.5 Learning styles** | Eg, identify apprentice's preferred learning styles | Coach and apprentice | Establish how preferred learning styles could be maximised in apprentice's learning | Six months |

*(continued)*

| Issue | Proposed actions | Responsibility for actions | Intended targets/ outcomes | Timing |
|---|---|---|---|---|
| **2.6 Deep and surface learning** | Eg, identify how deep learning could be fostered through apprentice's learning | Coach and apprentice | Maximise deep learning opportunities | Immediate |
| **2.7. Learning in organisations** | Eg, identify opportunities for learning and development both through work and off-the-job training | Coach, apprentice and other stakeholders | Exploit opportunities for learning and development | Immediate |
| **2.8 Current and emerging technologies** | Eg, update yourself and apprentice on emerging learning technologies that could be used in their occupational role | Coach and apprentice | Improve learning | Six months |

# 3 Mentoring processes

**CHAPTER CONTENT**

This chapter covers:



## INTRODUCTION

Mentoring's origins lie in Homer's *Odyssey* (eighth century BCE). In Homer's narrative, Mentor was given the task of caring for Telemachus while his father, Odysseus, was away. The 'care' Mentor provided was mostly spiritual and was designed to help Telemachus with his own self-development. The *Odyssey* recognised the importance of various types of guidance and provided Mentor with a 'chimaerian' (multifaceted) personality, enabling him to be a role model, a guide and a supportive friend while enjoying the wisdom of the goddess Athena, who could offer a balance in Telemachus' education and spiritual growth.

## 3.1 MENTORING ROLES AND MODELS

### *Activity 1*

***What kind of mentor are you?***

- Below is a series of roles mentors have described themselves as having. Considering your own relationship with your mentee, complete the pyramid below prioritising the six most important roles you feel you play. You can select these roles from the list below or add your own.

Advocate, appraiser, assessor, coach, colleague, consultant, counsellor, developer of talent, diagnoser, discipliner, expert, facilitator, friend, guardian, helper, instructor, leader, motivator, opener of doors, protector, role model, sponsor, teacher, trusted guide...

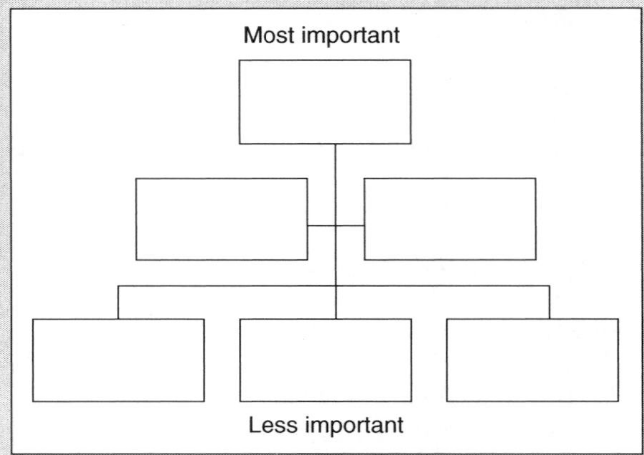


Figure 3a Activity 1

There are a number of continua for the key features or dimensions of what kind of mentor you are (Klasen and Clutterbuck, 2002).

- The first is the directive/non-directive continuum. This indicates the extent to which you tell/instruct/show your mentee what to do, rather than leave the initiative to them. So directive roles would be 'teacher' and 'instructor', with less directive roles being 'helper', 'opener of doors'.
- Second, there is the cognitive/emotional continuum. Do you see yourself as conveying knowledge/information as an 'expert', rather than attending to the more emotional dimensions of your mentee's development as 'counsellor' or 'friend'?
- Finally, do you see your roles as mainly active, as a 'discipliner' or 'assessor' rather acting more passively as 'colleague' or 'facilitator'?

### Activity 2

- Using the six roles specified in your pyramid, particularly the three most important, plot your position on each of these three continua.

Directive ..................................... Non-directive
Cognitive ..................................... Emotional
Active ..................................... Passive

## Mentoring metaphors

Another way of characterising your own operation as a mentor is by creating a metaphor that captures your style or approach to the task. The metaphor may be an animal such as a hawk (watches from a distance, is very sharp-eyed but is quick to swoop down when the time is necessary), a mother cat carrying a kitten around in her mouth (mentor taking all responsibility for learning), an adult bird (pushing the fledgling off the wall to enable it to fly – in at the deep end), a bull (in a china shop – goes charging in willy-nilly), a bee (works collaboratively and signposts where the pollen is) or a mother duck (her ducklings imprinting upon and blindly following her as the first moving stimulus they respond to after hatching).

Here are some metaphors used by participants on a mentoring course to describe the mentor journey:

> *[H]ow about mentoring as a tandem bicycle ride. Sometimes we are shouting 'Whee!!' as we cruise down the hill, feet stuck out to the side and hands in the air... and other times we are puffing and panting as we tackle some heavy uphill issues.*
>
> *Mentoring is very much like using a periscope with mentor and mentee serving as mirrors bouncing images back and forth with the ultimate goal of seeing higher and farther than a single mirror could ever do.*
>
> *The Mentor's Journey is a vine clinging to the trellis in a garden. There are twists and turns in its growth, yet it has the strength to lift up the leaves, provide food for continued growth, and nourish the fruit to full ripeness.*
>
> *The mentor/mentee relationship is a five-course meal. The appetizer is the mentor's self-awareness, so that he/she is able to facilitate an effective learning relationship. The salad is understanding the mentee's journey. The soup is the mentor in the role of the facilitator creating a supportive climate and the mentee's role of active partner who is diagnosing, planning, implementing and evaluating his/her own learning. The entrée is the learning process – where the mentee is self-directed and is responsible for his/her own learning that is goal determined. Dessert is realizing that mentor and mentee are co-learners who both benefit and grow from the relationship. And of course every good meal has lots of meaningful conversation involving questions, paraphrasing, summarizing and listening.*
>
> (Wikispaces, 2018a)

### *Activity 3*

- Create a metaphor that you feel accurately describes the kind of mentor you are and the relationship you have with your apprentice.

It should be added that there is no 'correct' set of mentor roles. Your own approach will depend on a number of factors: the nature of your occupational area and role and that of your mentee; your perception of the best way you can develop your mentee's occupational knowledge, skills and behaviours – what you can bring to the task; the nature and culture and size of your organisation; the needs of your mentee.

## 3.2 LEARNING FROM EXPERIENCE AND REFLECTIVE PRACTICE

It is likely that you will be working with your mentee in an occupational context in which much of their learning will be from experience. Kolb (1984) developed a four-stage cycle of experiential learning as shown in Figure 3b.

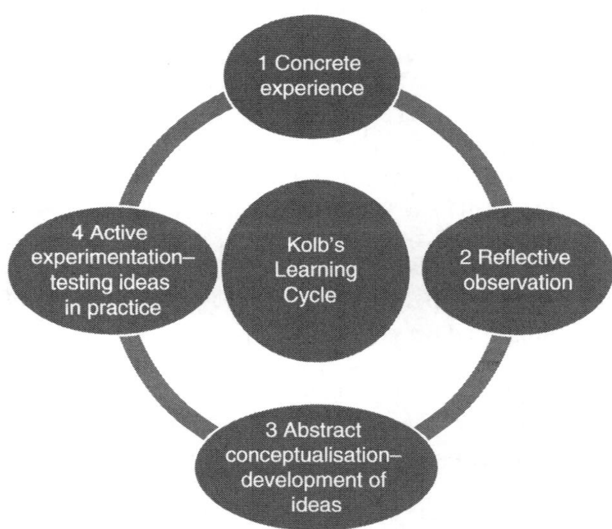


Figure 3b Kolb's four-stage cycle of experiential learning
Adapted from Kolb, 1984

1. The cycle begins with a vocational experience – for example, a plumbing apprentice joints a copper pipe under supervision (Stage 1).
2. The supervisor then determines, through questioning, how well the apprentice thinks they have done the job, what the difficulties were, and how it might have been done differently, encouraging the apprentice to think reflectively (Stage 2).

3. That night, the apprentice consults his course textbook about the different jointing methods, such as non-manipulative compression, manipulative compression, soldering capillary fitting and the contexts in which each method is suitable (Stage 3).
4. Back in the workplace, the apprentice gains practical experience of the different jointing methods, using the correct method in the correct circumstances and then tests the pipe (Stage 4).

### *Activity 4*

- Describe a learning episode your own mentee might go through in their current occupational context.

## Reflecting-in-action and reflecting-on-action

Schön (1983, 1991) describes one type of vocational knowledge as '*knowing-in-action*':

> *A tight-rope walker's know-how, for example, lies in, and is revealed by, the way he or she takes their trip across the wire, or a big league pitcher's know-how is in his way of pitching to a batter's weakness, changing his pace, or distributing his energies over the course of a game. There is nothing in common sense to make us say know-how consists in rules or plans which we entertain in the mind prior to action. Although we sometimes think before acting, it is also true that in much of the spontaneous behaviour of skilful practice we reveal a kind of knowing which does not stem from a prior intellectual operation.*
>
> (Schön, 1991, p 50)

This 'knowing-in-action' is similar to what Polyani (1967) described as '*tacit knowledge*', or knowledge we can't express in terms of the principles or evidence for what we know. Polyani gives examples from the recognition of faces: if we know a face, we can pick it out from among others or recognise different expressions, but we would not be able to specify how the recognition takes place.

As well as 'knowing-in-action', we may also be able to adjust our performance on the spot, responding to feedback as we go. Schön calls this '*reflecting-in-action*':

> *If common sense recognises knowing-in-action, it also recognises that we sometimes think about what we are doing. Phrases like 'thinking on your feet', 'keeping your wits about you' and 'learning by doing' suggest not only that we can think about doing but that we can think about doing something while doing it. Some of the most interesting examples of this process occur in the midst of a performance.*
>
> (Schön, 1991, p 55)

Schön contrasts reflection-in-action with reflection-on-action, the backward-looking review of practice, which would be similar to Kolb's Stage 2 'Reflective observation' above.

### Activity 5

- How could the ideas of reflecting-in-action and reflecting-on-action help you and your mentee improve their working practice?

## 3.3 THE MENTORING CYCLE

There is no ideal mentoring cycle. Particular cycles will depend on your view of learning and that of your mentee, your vocational area, your role and that of your mentee and the nature of the organisation in which you work. Figure 3c reflects Kolb's learning cycle. So an initial diagnostic meeting would explore the key issues regarding the apprentice's progress and development and the actions (or concrete experiences) necessary to enhance that progress and development. These might involve modelling: the apprentice observes the mentor at work and learns from their expert practice (this is 'Sitting-next-to-Nellie' and is the most common form of training generally associated with apprenticeships). The apprentice could also observe other staff with particular types of expertise. They could be offered hypothetical 'what would you do?' scenarios to test their versatility, creativity and technical know-how. They might be required to consult textbooks/handbooks to enhance their theoretical understanding of workplace tasks. Finally, they could be offered live feedback as they complete these workplace tasks.

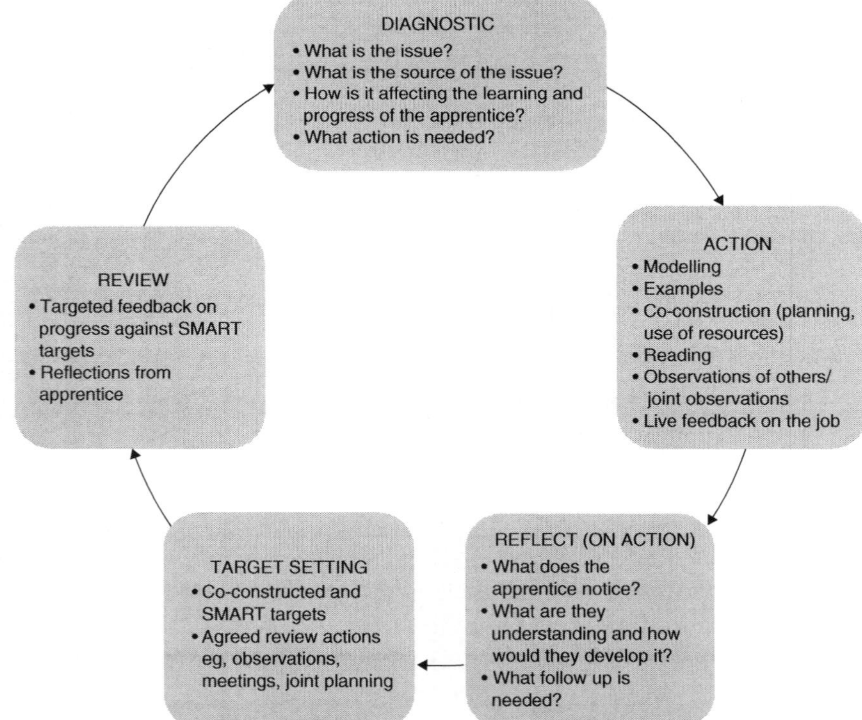


Figure 3c The mentoring cycle
Mentor Development Programme, Canterbury Christ Church University

The next stage of the cycle would consist of reflective observation on the actions and experiences the apprentice has had. What have they learned, what new knowledge and skills and behaviours have they acquired, what best practice have they observed, what new challenges have they recognised? And which further actions and experiences, if any, would be desirable?

Out of this reflective observation would come target-setting: what does the apprentice need to do to incorporate what they have learned into their vocational practice?

The most effective targets are SMART ones, where SMART stands for:

- **Specific** – the target needs to specify precisely the knowledge, skill level, behaviour required.
- **Measurable** – both mentor and mentee need to be able to assess clearly when the knowledge, skill level, behaviour has been demonstrated.
- **Achievable** – the target should be one which the mentee, at their stage of development, is capable of achieving
- **Realistic** – is the target achievable as part of the workplace role of the apprentice?
- **Timely** – giving the target a timeframe helps ensuring the aspects above are achieved.

## *Activity 6*

- In Table 3a is a series of targets. Assess how SMART these are where 1 is not very SMART and 5 is very SMART. The table is available at www.criticalpublishing.com/the-new-apprenticeships should you wish to complete it electronically. Suggested answers are given at the end of the book.

*Table 3a Activity 6*

| **Target** | **Occupational context** | **1** | **2** | **3** | **4** | **5** |
|---|---|---|---|---|---|---|
| 1. Improve punctuality. | Customer service in retail outlet L2 | | | | | |
| 2. Be able to lift client safely. | Caring role in care home L2 | | | | | |
| 3. Can effectively carry out all yard and field duties to include mucking out, skipping out, tidying and cleaning the yard, watering and feeding by Thursday 15 November. | Equine groom in racing yard L2 | | | | | |
| 4. Diagnose and rectify common faults in pillar taps by w/e 6 March. | Domestic plumbing apprentice L2 | | | | | |

*(continued)*

| Target | Occupational context | 1 | 2 | 3 | 4 | 5 |
|---|---|---|---|---|---|---|
| 5. Consult, prepare, plan and deliver skin care and make-up instruction, and evaluate the success of skin care and make-up instruction with customers. | Beauty and make-up consultant in a salon L2 | | | | | |
| 6. Monitor the weather and carry out specialist duties airside to ensure operational safety is maintained in low visibility and adverse weather conditions by end of apprenticeship. | Airside operator at airport L2 | | | | | |
| 7. Understand the characteristics of a variety of fabrics and their suitable application to construction by end year 1 of apprenticeship. | Bespoke tailor and cutter – L5 higher-level apprentice | | | | | |
| 8. Ensure ingredients are stored, prepared, cooked and presented to deliver a quality product that is safe for the consumer. | Chef de partie L3 | | | | | |
| 9. Identify ethical dilemmas, understand the implications and behave appropriately. Understand their legal responsibilities, both within the letter and the spirit of the law, as well as be aware of the procedures for reporting concerns over potentially unethical activities. Achieved by the end of this week. | Accountancy/ taxation professional L7 | | | | | |
| 10. Manage and conduct effective and efficient priority and high-volume investigations. Use initiative to diligently progress investigations, identifying, evaluating and following lines of enquiry to inform the possible initiation of criminal proceedings. Apply an investigative mind-set when decision-making. Present permissible evidence to authorities where required. Achieved by end of the apprenticeship. | Police constable – degree L6 | | | | | |

There would be a review of the mentee's progress against these SMART targets which would complete the cycle and lead to a further diagnostic meeting that would explore other key issues regarding the apprentice's progress and development and the actions (or concrete experiences) necessary to enhance that progress and development.

## 3.4 RECORDING LEARNER PROGRESS

If a learner progress report is going to support the mentoring cycle described above, it will need to answer the following questions.

- How far has the learner met the targets agreed in the last review?
- What progress has been made with regard to their behaviours, knowledge and skills?

- What new targets need to be agreed and when should they be achieved?
- What actions are needed by which parties to enable the apprentice to achieve these targets?

Although the standards below are to be met by the time the end-point assessment is carried out, an ongoing indication of how far the apprentice is working towards these standards, ascertained through formative assessment to be fed back and fed forward to the apprentice, is an important part of your role as a mentor.

## Scenario

Maisie is 92 years old and lives alone in sheltered accommodation. Her husband died 15 years ago and she has no children. Her younger sister lives a half-hour drive away and visits once a month. Her self-contained flat is one of 24 and a manager is on site 9–5 Monday to Friday. There is a strong community ethos and the majority of residents look out for each other and meet regularly with the manager to discuss community issues. Maisie doesn't engage much with meetings or any organised entertainment but enjoys the visits of residents who pop in regularly.

Maisie recently had a fall and was hospitalised. She was discharged from hospital with a care plan in place. Maisie is dependent on carers to help her in the mornings with washing and dressing and again at night when she goes to bed. Maisie has her meals delivered and is able to use the microwave to heat these up but needs help with domestic work such as keeping the kitchen clean and vacuuming. Maisie wears hearing aids.

The mentor, Kiran McGregor, accompanies and observes a healthcare support worker level 2 apprentice, Danielle Downer, carrying out a client home visit to Maisie. Their mentor observation feedback summary is below.

## Mentor observation feedback summary

Prior to the observation we had agreed that I would focus the observation on the following:

- communication in the home setting (1);
- health interventions in the home setting (4.3);
- moving and handling in the home setting (4.4).

You provided me with sufficient background detail and the context of the work you were undertaking and that this would be in the client's home and their needs would be recorded in their care plan. You provided me with a copy of this prior to the observation and this was up to date. You provided copies of previous observations and I was able to access these through the online evidence portal. We agreed that verbal feedback would be brief as you need to travel to your next client/patient after the observation. I have agreed to send you an electronic copy of the written observation for your evidence record and to carry out a full discussion to support your development in the next seven working days. The observation report will be uploaded to the online assessment portal where you, your apprentice provider, employer and mentor have password protected access.

At 8.30am we meet in the car park and enter the flat together. Your client is in bed and your greeting is cheerful. You explain my presence and reassure her.

You explained the purpose of the observer's presence to your client, reminding her of a previous discussion and gaining consent – you reassured her. After you had helped your client out of bed, you asked me to sit in a chair by the window so you could carry out your tasks.

Your client needs to use the bathroom and you help her out of bed using appropriate techniques. Your client uses a walking frame and you escort her to the bathroom where she also has her morning wash. Everything in the bathroom is accessible and your client is able to wash herself with some independence, which you encourage. I was able to hear you and your client and observe most of your interactions, while avoiding the bathroom for privacy and dignity.

After helping your client prepare her breakfast, you continued to talk to your client while checking over the bathroom and kitchen areas. You also made her bed.

You clearly have a good rapport with your client and she was pleased to see you. You are respectful in your practice. You provided opportunities for her to maintain some independence and this is an area of strength.

Although your client made some responses to your voice when you were not in the room, you were unable to notice if your client had responded appropriately to your comments and I wonder if she was able to hear you properly. You did not check. Your client was fiddling with her hearing aids. These do need checking regularly and you do need to check if your client can hear you well enough to participate in conversations.

Well done.

## A record of learner progress

Subsequently, Kiran McGregor completes a record of learner progress related to the standard's criteria feeding in relevant aspects of the observation feedback (Table 3b). **Bold text** in the Comments column suggests satisfactory achievement and *italicised text* potential targets for the future. An actual completed report would show evidence from other sources.

*Table 3b Learner progress report: healthcare support worker level 2*

**Mentor: Kiran McGregor**
**Apprentice: Danielle Downer**
Date: 5 September 2018

| **Targets brought forward from previous review meeting on............** | **Progress achieved against targets** |
|---|---|
| 1. Identify opportunities for supporting individuals with daily activities in the home (2) | Target met through observation |
| 2. Further develop communication skills in a wide range of settings (1) | Partially met – additional evidence and action required |
| 3. Moving and handling individuals in the home (4.4) | Target met through observation |
| Progress achieved against standards | |
| Behaviours<br><br>You will treat people with dignity, respecting individuals' diversity, beliefs, culture, values, needs, privacy and preferences; show respect and empathy for those you work with; have the courage to challenge areas of concern and work to best practice; be adaptable, reliable and consistent; show discretion; show resilience and self-awareness. | |

| **Skill** | **You will be able to:** | **You will know and understand:** | **Comments:** |
|---|---|---|---|
| 1 Communication | • communicate effectively with individuals, their families, carers and healthcare practitioners using a range of techniques, keeping information confidential<br>• handle information (record, report and store information) related to individuals in line with local and national policies | • why it is important to communicate effectively at work<br>• how to communicate with individuals that have specific language needs or wishes<br>• ways to make yourself understood<br>• how to reduce problems with communication<br>• legislation, policies and local ways of working (about handling information)<br>• how to keep information confidential<br>• why it is important to record and store patient information securely and what to do if you think information is not secure | **You communicated with your client well initially. You continued to speak to her when you were in the kitchen.**<br>*How do you know that your client heard what you were saying?*<br>*(see target)* |

| | | | |
|---|---|---|---|
| 2 Health intervention | • support individuals with long term conditions, frailty and end of life (6) care<br>• identify and respond to signs of pain or discomfort<br>• promote physical health and wellbeing of individuals<br>• assist with an individual's overall comfort and wellbeing<br>• support individuals with activities of daily living<br>• recognise deteriorations in health, long term conditions, physiological measurements, skin integrity and appropriately report any changes in physical health needs as appropriate | • how to do routine clinical tasks (eg, check blood pressure, temperature, weight etc) delegated from a registered nurse or other healthcare professional<br>• the signs and symptoms of a person who is experiencing pain or discomfort<br>• how to promote a person's physical health and wellbeing<br>• how to support a person's comfort and wellbeing<br>• the importance of hydration, nutrition and food safety<br>• what the activities of daily living are and which ones you are expected to support in your role<br>• the signs of a person whose health and wellbeing is deteriorating; and how to report changes and deterioration | **You encouraged independence with day-to-day tasks.**<br>**You checked that your client had been eating her meals and helped her prepare her breakfast.**<br>**You monitored the contents of the fridge and checked her milk and soft drinks and basic supplies.**<br>**You recorded relevant information in the care plan.** |
| 2.1 Person-centred care and support | • demonstrate what it means in practice to provide person centred care and support | • what it means to give 'person-centred care and support'<br>• why it is important to get consent, even when it is difficult<br>• why it is important to get people actively involved in their own care<br>• why it is important to give people choices about their care; and why treating people as valuable and unique individuals makes a big difference in how they feel | |

| | | | |
|---|---|---|---|
| 2.2 Dementia, cognitive issues, mental health | • promote mental health and wellbeing<br>• recognise limitations in mental capacity and respond appropriately<br>• recognise and respond to signs of poor mental health, for example dementia, depression, anxiety or other cognitive issues<br>• recognise and report any deterioration in an individual's mental health | • the main forms of mental ill-health and their impact on people's lives; and how to promote mental health and wellbeing<br>• the possible signs of limitations in mental capacity and what to do when you notice them<br>• the possible signs of mental health, dementia and learning disability in people<br>• why depression, delirium and the normal ageing process may be mistaken for dementia<br>• the importance of early diagnosis in relation to dementia and other cognitive issues<br>• how to report changes or deterioration | **You encourage and support your client's independence noting that she is pleased when she completes a task herself.** |
| 2.3 Basic life support | • perform basic life support for individuals using appropriate resuscitation techniques and equipment | • how to perform basic life support | |
| 2.4 Physiological measurements | • undertake a range of physiological measurements using the appropriate equipment including height, weight, temperature, pulse, breathing rate and blood pressure | • the range of physiological states that can be measured including body temperature, weight, height, blood pressure, pulse and breathing rate<br>• the normal range of physiological measurements | |
| 3 Personal and people development | • take responsibility for, prioritise and reflect on your own actions and work<br>• work as part of a team, seeking help and guidance when you are not sure | • your role and the responsibilities and duties of your job<br>• why it is important to work in ways that have been agreed by your employer and to follow standards/codes of conduct | |

| | | | |
|---|---|---|---|
| | • maintain and further develop your own skills and knowledge through development activities<br>• maintain evidence of your personal development and actively prepare for and participate in appraisal | • working relationships and the importance of working well with other people<br>• who or where to go for help and support about anything related to your work<br>• the importance of personal development and how to reflect on your work; how to create a personal development plan | |
| 4 Health, safety and security | • maintain a safe and healthy working environment take appropriate action in response to incidents or emergencies following local guidelines | • legislation, policies and local ways of working which relate to health and safety at work<br>• your responsibilities, and the responsibilities of others, relating to health and safety at work; what to do in situations that could cause harm to themselves and others; how to handle hazardous materials and substances<br>• what to do when there is an accident or sudden illness | |
| 4.1 Duty of care | • follow the principles for implementing a duty of care, always acting in the best interest of individuals to ensure they do not come to harm | • the meaning of 'duty of care' and why it is important<br>• what support is available when you come across a difficult situation or when someone makes a complaint | |
| 4.2 Safeguarding | • follow the principles of safeguarding and protection | • legislation, policies and local ways of working about 'safeguarding' and protection from abuse | |

| | | | |
|---|---|---|---|
| | | • the signs of abuse and what to do if you suspect abuse<br>• and how to reduce the chances of abuse as much as possible | |
| 4.3 Infection prevention and control | • use a range of techniques for infection prevention and control including waste management, hand washing and the use of Personal Protective Equipment (PPE) | • legislation, policies and local ways of working that help to prevent infection; the meaning of 'risk' and 'risk assessment'<br>• the importance of good personal hygiene and hand washing<br>• how to select the right PPE (such as gloves, aprons and masks)<br>• how infections start and spread; the importance of cleaning, disinfecting and maintaining a clean workplace to reduce the risk and spread of infection<br>• the meaning of 'antimicrobial resistance' | **You were in a clean uniform and washed your hands before and after your visit.** |
| 4.4 Moving and handling | • move and position individuals, equipment and other items safely | • why people and objects need to be moved safely<br>• how to move and position people safely<br>• how to move and handle equipment and other objects safely<br>• agreed ways of working when moving people and know how to identify any risks | **You helped your client out of bed using the appropriate techniques.** |
| 5 Equality and diversity | • follow the principles of equality, diversity and inclusion | • equality and diversity legislation, policies and local ways of working<br>• why equality is important and how discrimination can happen at work | |

| Targets to be achieved | Timing |
|---|---|
| 1. Recognise when your client is unable to hear you (1) | At next visit |
| 2. Undertake physiological measurements in an appropriate care setting (2.4) | Next observation |
| 3. Further develop knowledge and skills in infection prevention and control (4.3) | Next observation |
| **Actions needed to achieve these targets** | **By whom?** |
| 1. Always check if your client can understand what you are saying by seeking an appropriate response. Check if hearing aids are working properly, record and report to the appropriate personnel (1) | |
| 2. Identify a suitable patient/service user and demonstrate skills and understanding through care plans/records (2.4) | Apprentice and mentor discussion |
| 3. Plan for skills development in a suitable setting (4.3) | Apprentice |
| Signed......Kiran McGregor..........................................................Mentor | |
| Signed......Danielle Downer.........................................................Apprentice | |

### *Activity 7*

- Design your own learner progress report.

Table 3b is available at www.criticalpublishing.com/the-new-apprenticeships should you wish to adapt it.

## 3.5 MANAGING AND MAINTAINING THE MENTOR–MENTEE RELATIONSHIP

### *Activity 8*

Below is a series of features of the mentor–mentee relationship considered to be desirable.

- Before reading on, group these features according to whether you think they relate to:
  - a) qualities of the mentor–mentee relationship;
  - b) aspects of the mentoring process;
  - c) roles, responsibilities and boundaries

- mentor availability
- honesty and openness
- regularity of meetings
- mutual learning and collaboration
- informality
- flexibility
- enthusiasm for learning and development
- rules of confidentiality
- having a set agenda for meetings
- non-dominance
- empathy
- supporting the apprentice in maintaining good relationships
- understanding what is expected of mentor and mentee
- responsibility for recording meetings
- role modelling/leading by example
- good rapport
- effective time management
- giving structured and constructive feedback
- target setting
- brokering opportunities
- enable and encourage self-evaluation and improvement
- respect and trust
- suitable meeting environment
- constructive questioning.

## Qualities of the mentor–mentee relationship

We saw in Section 3.1 that each mentor is likely to have their own individual style, according to which mentor roles they feel it important for them to play. However, there are certain qualities of the mentor–mentee relationship that are more likely to enhance the mentoring experience. It is important that the relationship is honest and open. It is unlikely that a mentee will grow and develop unless their mentor is clear and open about what they are doing well and less well and what they need to do to improve. Equally, the mentee needs to feel confident that they are able to be honest about their progress with the mentor. Such openness is closely linked to mutual respect and trust. Neither mentor nor mentee is going to be open and honest unless they both have the respect and trust of the other party and can give this in return. Closely related to openness, respect and trust is empathy – the capacity to step into other people's shoes. It is important that the old hand is able to recall the challenges to the novice, which may for them be many years in the past. Empathy is one aspect of rapport, facilitating better communication between mentor and mentee. Although there are formal aspects of the mentoring relationship (considered below), an informal relationship is more likely to foster the positive aspects already discussed. Part of this informality should be a flexibility on both parts, not rigid adherence to a formal process. Non-dominance on the part of mentors is also important: although there is a place for instruction ('that's the way to do it'), mentees generally learn most effectively when they play a more active role. Enthusiasm for the learning and development process on both parts is important; indeed, taking the view that mentoring is a process of mutual learning and collaboration may be the most productive approach, with the mentor considering how they are benefiting themselves from the process in terms of their own development. Teachers often note how, in mentoring student teachers, they are led to consider and review their own practice when helping a newcomer develop theirs.

## Aspects of the mentoring process

One of the most important features mentees often claim they prize most in their mentors is their availability – 'They were always there for me'. And, conversely, a mentor's lack of availability was often seen as a key factor in the breakdown of mentor–mentee relationships. This is a major challenge in a busy organisation when both parties have limited time. One way of overcoming this challenge is to set a regular meeting time. Mentoring will not, of course, be limited to this meeting: the carpenter with one apprentice will be engaged in informal mentoring throughout the working day. However, a slot does need to be set aside for a regular meeting for a similar period of time and with a set agenda. This ensures consistency from one meeting to the next, allowing for structured feedback and the setting and monitoring of targets.

## Roles, responsibilities and boundaries

Having a clear idea about what is expected from each as part of their relationship is an important element in maintaining it. Confusion over this can be frustrating and demotivating for both. Whose responsibility is it to record the meetings, for example? You may wish to formalise these responsibilities in a written 'contract', which you can both refer to should the need arise. This contract should specify the rules of confidentiality underpinning the relationship. These will clarify what information about the trainee will be given to third parties, for example. There are many contract templates available and your training provider should be able to help select an appropriate one. Indeed, this contract should be related to the contractual agreement in place between employer, provider and apprentice. A high level of professionalism or craftsmanship on the part of the mentor is a key element in earning the mentee's respect and modelling is an important and effective responsibility the mentor has in inducting the mentee into working practice. However, care should be taken to ensure there is flexibility in this modelling so that the mentor is not simply producing a 'mini-me'!

## Twelve habits of the toxic mentor

Finally, David Clutterbuck (nd) light-heartedly describes *Twelve Habits of the Toxic Mentor*.

1. *Start from the point of view that you – from your vast experience and broader perspective – know better than the mentee what's in his or her interest.*
2. *Be determined to share your wisdom with them – whether they want it or not; remind them frequently how much they still have to learn.*
3. *Decide what you and the mentee will talk about and when; change dates and themes frequently to prevent complacency sneaking in.*
4. *Do most of the talking; check frequently that they are paying attention.*
5. *Make sure they understand how trivial their concerns are compared to the weighty issues you have to deal with.*
6. *Remind the mentee how fortunate they are to have your undivided attention.*
7. *Neither show nor admit any personal weaknesses; expect to be their role model in all aspects of career development and personal values.*
8. *Never ask them what they should expect of you – how would they know anyway?*
9. *Demonstrate how important and well connected you are by sharing confidential information they don't need (or want) to know.*
10. *Discourage any signs of levity or humour – this is a serious business and should be treated as such.*
11. *Take them to task when they don't follow your advice.*
12. *Never, never admit that this could be a learning experience for you, too.*

### *Activity 9*

- Considering: a) qualities of the mentor–mentee relationship; b) aspects of the mentoring process; and c) roles, responsibilities and boundaries, evaluate how effective your mentor–mentee relationship is.

## 3.6 MENTORING AND COACHING

Mentoring and coaching are not mutually exclusive: a mentor who has a long-term mentoring relationship with an apprentice may use coaching techniques in the short term, for example. The emphasis in mentoring, however, is on mentor and mentee identifying learning aims, whereas in coaching the coach helps the coachee clarify their own learning aims. Coaching is non-judgemental and solution-focused whereas mentoring often involves a degree of assessment or appraisal. In the business world, coaching has often been selected as an approach to developing managers, company stars or high fliers. However, in other vocational fields – teacher education, for example – coaching is often used for those undertaking initial qualifications as well as for continuing professional development. The key distinctions between mentoring and coaching are set out in Table 3c.

*Table 3c Distinctions between mentoring and coaching*

| Mentoring | Coaching |
|---|---|
| • Usually long-term | • Usually short-term (but note athletics coach, swimming coach) |
| • Mentor will have knowledge, skills, performance capacity at least equal to and usually superior to mentee | • Coach does not need knowledge, skills, performance capacity of coachee (note – football coach!) |
| • Mentors concerned with acquiring new knowledge and skills | • Coaches concerned with improving performance |
| • More relationship-oriented | • More task-oriented – focusing on a particular skill/performance, area for improvement |
| • Often informal | • Often structured and more formal |

One of the key coaching strategies is the specific questioning by the coach of the coachee. Carole Pemberton (2006) recommends the following approaches to questioning:

- Ask 'what' questions such as 'What is happening right now?' 'What would be a good outcome?' 'What are you most worried about?'
- Use 'how' questions: 'How would you like it to be different?' 'How would you know if things were improving?'
- 'When' questions are used to identify evidence of desired change and to build commitment to doing something differently 'When do you feel engaged in your work?' 'When did you last feel positively challenged by your work?'

## Scenario

Students on a university Postgraduate Certificate in Education are offered coaching after each assessment point. Aretha Macdonald is a PGCE student placed at City College. Her specialist subject is psychology and she has a 2.1 BSc from University College Westminster. At her first assessment point, she self-assessed as follows.

### Strengths

1. Enthusiasm and passion for my subject
2. I have a lively and engaging teaching personality
3. I have a respectful approach to my learners

## Areas for development

1. Manage difficult behaviour better
2. Develop time management skills
3. Develop clearer task setting so that learners understand what is required of them
4. Develop planning to include the needs of all learners across a range of abilities, stretching and challenging all learners

Aretha and her coach have a pre-observation meeting and then a meeting after the observation. This is how the pre-observation meeting went:

**Coach:** *Aretha, I noticed in your self-assessment that there are a number of areas for development you identified.*

**Aretha:** *That's right.*

**Coach:** *Are there any that you feel are more urgent, that you feel are priorities?*

**Aretha:** *Managing difficult behaviour, definitely.*

**Coach:** *Why 'definitely'?*

**Aretha:** *I guess it's what winds me up most easily. I mean, if I can't control the group, I can't teach them really, can I?*

**Coach:** *OK, so what happens in your lessons? What behaviours wind you up?*

**Aretha:** *Well, students chatting privately to each other while I'm talking.*

**Coach:** *So, what bothers you about that?*

**Coach:** *Well, it's rude, isn't it? And, sometimes their body language, well they seem to be talking about me.*

**Coach:** *OK, anything else?*

**Aretha:** *Yes, well, some of the learners take me on when I make specific points. It's like, they know I'm a student so what do I know about anything?*

**Coach:** *How do they take you on? Give me an example.*

**Aretha:** *So, I'm trying to explain the role and interaction of the ego, super ego and id for Freud and one boy starts to say I've got it wrong – it's not what his textbook says and it's not what their normal teacher has said either and he's got the notes to prove it.*

**Coach:** *OK, anything else?*

**Aretha:** *Yes, I'll put them into groups and give them a task and before long they'll say they're bored with what I've given them to do... I mean – they're A level students. You'd think they'd be better motivated!*

**Coach:** *So, what is it you want from this coaching – what would count as success?*

**Aretha:** *I suppose, just to look at some practical strategies for dealing with the behaviour I've mentioned. I'm not looking to be a behaviour expert overnight – but just the beginnings of dealing with it...*

### *Activity 10*

- In the coaching conversation above, consider how the coach went about preparing for the observation and post-observation conversation before going on to read the comment on the scenario below.

## Comment on scenario

First, the coach has used Aretha's own self-assessment to identify the aspects of her performance she wishes to improve. She is more likely to be motivated to succeed since these are her choices. And she has identified three examples of difficult behaviour commonly experienced by student or novice teachers: low-level disruption undermining the activity and the teacher's authority; intellectual interjection challenging the teacher's expertise and authority; and refusal to engage with learning activities. The coach has probably also picked up on some of Aretha's expectations and assumptions that may need addressing if she is to move forward: the assumption that she controls the group and *then* teaches them, rather than exerts different types and strategies of control through the lesson; the assumption that the learners' conversations are about her; the assumption that all A level students should be motivated at all times; the assumption that the learners' 'boredom' results from poor motivation. The coach has also elicited from Aretha what practical, reasonable outcomes she wants for the coaching process.

## Post-observation conversation

This was the post-observation conversation.

**Coach:** *So Aretha, let's focus on those specific aspects of behaviour management you were concerned about. How did things work out today, do you think?*

**Aretha:** *Well, there were still students chatting during my presentation.*

**Coach:** *That's right – and how did you handle them?*

**Aretha:** *I ignored it.*

**Coach:** *Which of course is a perfectly valid strategy. Were you happy with that?*

**Aretha:** *No, I found it distracting.*

**Coach:** *What were the other options?*

**Aretha:** *I could have stopped – made an issue of it, made an example of them.*

**Coach:** *And what are the risks with that approach?*

**Aretha:** *I suppose... it makes it into a big deal.*

**Coach:** *And could end up doing exactly what they might have wanted – gained your attention, even undermining your presentation by stopping you? What else might you have done?*

**Aretha:** *Ask them to be quiet without making a big deal of it – low key, light tone of voice and then move on quickly?*

**Coach:** *Try that next time? And you had the same student challenging your key definitions, didn't you? You moved on quickly, didn't you? What else could you have done?*

**Aretha:** *I suppose moving on like that shows he's spooked me.*

**Coach:** *Yes...*

**Aretha:** *I could have thanked him for his point and perhaps used it as a springboard for further discussion.*

**Coach:** *How?*

**Aretha:** *Well, I could have referred to the rest of the group – asked them for their views.*

**Coach:** *Ask the audience?*

**Aretha:** *Yes.*

**Coach:** *Now, you had your group refusals to engage again, didn't you? You know, I listened to the group near me... they didn't actually know what you wanted them to do.*

**Aretha:** *Really, they didn't say.*

**Coach:** *Can be quite hard for students to tell you that, you know.*

**Aretha:** *So that ties in with another area of development, doesn't it – clearer task setting?*

**Coach:** *Yes, so behaviour management isn't just about control and interventions – it's to do with your entire teaching repertoire. So stuff to try next time round?*

**Aretha:** *Yes.*

**Coach:** *Good.*

The coach focused on highly practical aspects of Aretha's performance as identified in the pre-observation conversation. They didn't criticise how or what Aretha did but asked her to consider alternative strategies and their possible consequences. They used their experience and position as an observer to confirm the group behaviour Aretha had not seen that might have made her act differently. They raised Aretha's awareness of the interconnectedness of aspects of her teaching.

## 3.7 SAFETY, HEALTH AND THE ENVIRONMENT

As an apprenticeship is a work-based training programme, a good starting point for mentor and apprentice will be health and safety and the working environment.

### Scenario

Below is a short report of a health and safety related site inspection/learning walk by an apprentice and their mentor.

**Apprenticeship context**: The property maintenance operative at level 2 caretaker or premises manager in the education sector.

**Premises**: A large two form entry primary school with a pre-school and a Children's Centre.

**The role profile explains that**: The primary role of a property maintenance operative is to optimise property condition and quality and to ensure the building is kept in a safe working condition. Property maintenance operatives need to maintain a high level of quality, providing maximum satisfaction to customers, clients, guests and team. They will understand the mechanism of buildings including electrical, plumbing, plant, safety systems and equipment. They will provide first and immediate response to fault finding, while maximising quality and ensuring cost-effectiveness. They will ensure prevention of major damage that could result in extensive costs and minimise reactive intervention. Apprenticeship reference: ST0171, Version: 1.1, Date updated: 03/05/2018, Approved for delivery: 26 March 2015, Route: Construction, Typical duration: 12 months.

For professional recognition, the apprentice will be recognised by the British Institute of Facilities Management (BIFM) providing Associate Membership for the apprentice while studying.

### Short report of a health and safety related site inspection/learning walk by an apprentice and their mentor

During an arranged meeting with the mentor (site manager) the apprentice undertook a one-hour induction activity focusing on what an apprentice needs to know. Through a site inspection and applying the Health and Safety Toolbox the apprentice was able to find out more about the management of health and safety in this particular organisation and their place as an employee. Through this activity, and discussion with the mentor, the apprentice was able to find out that not all elements in the toolbox were relevant. Through covering the relevant responsibilities for self and others including electrical safety, fire safety, gas safety, water safety, harmful substances, manual handling, personal and protective equipment (PPE), slips and trip hazards, working at heights and workplace transport, the apprentice was able to ask questions and the mentor was able to provide answers to these questions.

In managing and planning for healthy and safety the apprentice was able to know that there is a policy in place.

There were risk assessments to control risk.

There is a mechanism for reporting accidents and subsequent investigations.

The site is occupied by multiple organisations – the pre-school and the Children's Centre are managed separately from the school.

Looking at the 'Knowledge, skills and behaviours' for this apprenticeship standard, the apprentice and the mentor can link this activity to beginning to understand the core technical competencies/skills and knowledge/understanding required. Workplace activities and tasks the mentor has planned for the apprentice can then provide opportunities that enable the apprentice to collect evidence for the behaviours and skills required, for example, through problem solving and the ability to take responsibility and own the work set.

## Activity 11

- Using the Health and Safety Executive's *The Health and Safety Toolbox* (at the time of writing, this was available on the HSE website at: www.hse.gov.uk/pubns/books/hsg268.htm, and could be downloaded free), consider what your apprentice needs to know/understand, be able to do and have (eg, specialist equipment) in relation to their occupational role. Clearly, some of the topics in Table 3d will be relevant or not according to that role. You may wish to complete this exercise together with your apprentice.

*Table 3d Activity 11*

| TOPIC | What your apprentice needs to:<br>• know<br>• be able to do<br>• have | How you are going to help them achieve this |
|---|---|---|
| **1 How to manage health and safety**<br>Planning for health and safety<br>Writing a health and safety policy<br>Controlling the risks<br>Accidents and investigations<br>Multi-occupancy workplaces<br>Deciding who will help you with your duties<br>Consulting your employees<br>Providing training and information<br>Providing supervision<br>First aid<br>Emergency procedures<br>Reporting accidents, incidents and diseases<br>The health and safety law poster<br>Safety signs<br>Insurance<br>Inspectors and the law | | |
| **2 Your organisation**<br>Ergonomics (study of people's efficiency in their working environment) and human factors<br>Shift work and fatigue<br>Health surveillance<br>Work-related stress<br>Drugs and alcohol<br>Violence at work | | |
| **3 Your workers**<br>Your responsibilities<br>New and expectant mothers<br>Agency/temporary workers<br>New to the job and young workers<br>Migrant workers<br>Lone workers<br>Homeworkers<br>Transient workers | | |

| | | |
|---|---|---|
| People with disabilities<br>Contractors | | |
| **4 Your workplace**<br>A safe place of work<br>Designing workstations<br>Display screen equipment | | |
| **5 Electrical safety**<br>Maintenance<br>When is someone competent to do electrical work?<br>Key points to remember<br>Overhead electric lines<br>Underground cables | | |
| **6 Fire safety**<br>General fire safety hazards<br>Dangerous substances that cause fire and explosion | | |
| **7 Gas safety**<br>Who is competent to work on gas fittings? | | |
| **8 Harmful substances**<br>How to carry out a COSHH risk assessment<br>Maintain controls<br>Simple checks to control dust and mist<br>Ventilation<br>Simple checks to prevent skin damage<br>Workplace exposure limits<br>Are your controls adequate?<br>Micro-organisms<br>Asbestos<br>Lead | | |
| **9 Machinery, plant and equipment**<br>Why is machinery safety important?<br>Plant and equipment maintenance<br>Safe lifting by machine<br>Vehicle repair | | |
| **10 Manual handling**<br>Why is dealing with manual handling important?<br>Practical tips for good lifting technique | | |
| **11 Noise**<br>Why is dealing with noise important?<br>Do I have a noise problem? | | |

*(continued)*

| TOPIC | What your apprentice needs to:<br>• know<br>• be able to do<br>• have | How you are going to help them achieve this |
|---|---|---|
| How can I control noise?<br>Choosing quieter equipment and machinery<br>When should personal hearing protection be used?<br>Detecting damage to hearing | | |
| **12 Personal protective equipment (PPE)**<br>Why is PPE important?<br>Selection and use<br>Maintenance<br>Types of PPE you can use<br>Emergency equipment | | |
| **13 Pressure equipment**<br>Why is pressure equipment safety important?<br>Assess the risks<br>Basic precautions<br>Written scheme of examination | | |
| **14 Radiations**<br>What are the main types of radiation?<br>The hazards<br>Dos and don'ts of radiation safety | | |
| **15 Slips and trips**<br>Why is dealing with slips and trips important?<br>Slips and Trips eLearning Package (STEP) | | |
| **16 Vibration**<br>Why is dealing with vibration important?<br>How can I reduce hand-arm vibration?<br>How can I reduce whole-body vibration? | | |
| **17 Working at height**<br>Dos and don'ts of working at height | | |
| **18 Working in confined spaces**<br>Dos and don'ts of working in confined spaces | | |
| **19 Workplace transport**<br>Safe site<br>Safe vehicle<br>Safe driver | | |

## 3.8 YOUR ORGANISATION AND YOUR PARTNERS IN TRAINING

The nature of the organisation you and your apprentice work in is likely to affect the mentoring relationship you have. A key aspect of your organisation is its culture. Handy describes the key determinants of an organisation's culture:

> *In organisations there are deep-set beliefs about the way work should be organised, the way authority should be exercised, people rewarded, people controlled. What are the degrees of formalization required? How much planning and how far ahead? What combination of obedience and initiative is looked for in workers? Do work hours matter, or dress, or personal eccentricities? What about expense accounts, and secretaries, stock options and incentives? Do committees control, or individuals? Are there rules and procedures or only results? The kinds of people it employs, the length and height of their career aspirations, their status in society, degree of mobility, level of education, will all be reflections of the culture.*
>
> (Handy, 1993, p 181)

Handy goes on to describe four main types of culture: power, role, task and person.

### Power culture

Organisations with a power culture resemble spiders' webs, says Handy, with the controlling spider at the centre of the web wielding the power. The spider may be an individual or a small number of like-minded individuals – a controlling elite or dictatorship.

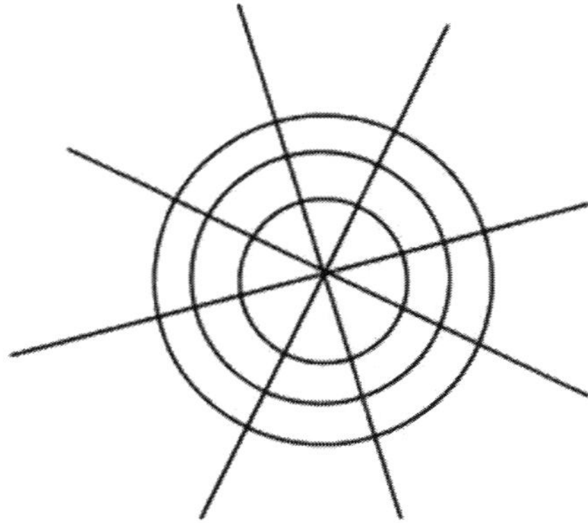

Figure 3d Power culture

Control is exercised by summoning individuals to the centre of the web or by forays across the web: the spider has rapid access to all parts of the web. The organisation puts its faith in individuals rather than committees. These are organisations that can respond rapidly to change, depending on the capacity of those at the centre. Individuals attracted to and appointed to the organisation will be similar in their operation to the spider. They will be self-starting, power-oriented risk-takers who thrive in a competitive environment. Successful performance is judged by results alone. Small, successful entrepreneurial organisations are most likely to have power cultures.

- Mentor models most likely to thrive in power cultures: role model, developer of talent, facilitator, sponsor, opener of doors.
- Mentor models least likely to succeed in power cultures: discipliner, instructor, teacher, expert.

## Role culture or bureaucracy

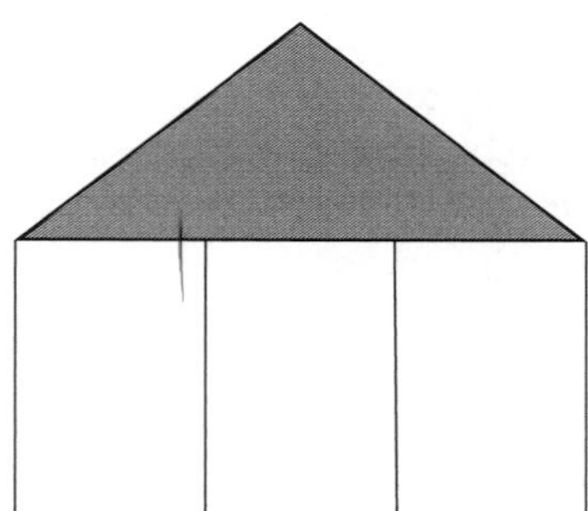

Figure 3e Role culture

The symbolic structure of a role culture is, for Handy, the Greek temple. The strength of this culture lies in its pillars which might comprise the finance department, purchasing department, production department, and so on. Both the work of the pillars and their interaction are controlled by procedures for roles, eg, job descriptions; procedures for communications, eg, set standard forms; rules for the settlement of disputes, eg, grievance procedures. The pillars are co-ordinated at the top by a small band of senior managers – the pediment. The occupational role or post or job is more important than the individual. The role culture thrives on a stable environment in which rules, procedures and policies work and apply ('we do it this way'). Role culture would be dominant in the civil service, BBC, motor and oil industries, life insurance companies and retail banking. Role culture offers predictability, the security of established practices and routines. It offers the opportunities to climb the pillars, but is not for the power-oriented individuals who want control of their own work and practice.

- Mentor models most likely to thrive in role cultures: appraiser, assessor, consultant, diagnoser, discipliner, instructor, teacher.
- Mentor models least likely to succeed in role cultures: coach, counsellor, developer of talent, facilitator, helper.

## Task culture

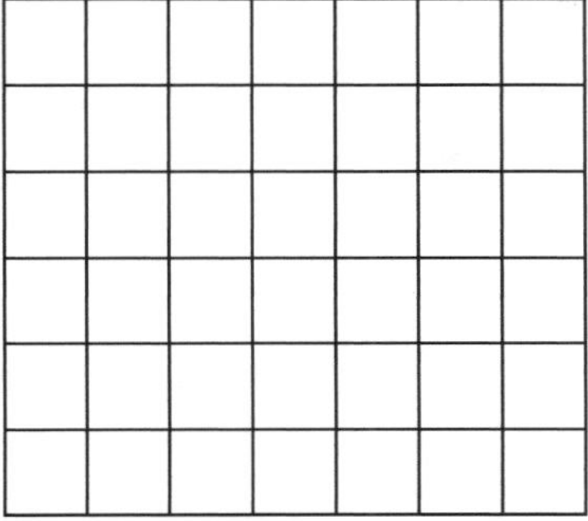

Figure 3f Task culture

The task culture is job- or project-oriented and is best represented as a net or matrix. For each job or task, a team is put together from across the network comprising individuals with particular specialisms. These teams can then be abandoned when the job is completed, then can be reformed or new teams assembled for new projects. The outcome of the team's work takes precedence over individual objectives. These cultures are extremely adaptable, with individuals having a high degree of control over their work. Handy gives the account departments of advertising agencies or a product group of a marketing department as examples of task cultures.

- Mentor models most likely to thrive in task cultures: colleague, consultant, helper, trusted guide.
- Mentor models least likely to succeed in task cultures: instructor, teacher.

## Person culture

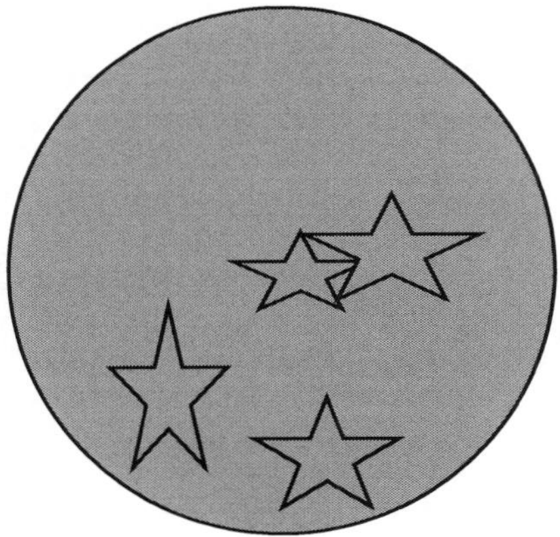

Figure 3g Person culture

The structure of a person culture is minimal but might best be described, Handy thinks, as a cluster or perhaps a galaxy of individual stars. For the person culture, the individual is all-important and any structure is there to serve the individuals within it. Barristers' chambers and architects' practices are good examples of person cultures, as are more recently formed social media companies and those devoted to producing emerging technologies. The life-blood of the latter is innovation and the person culture is characterised by its key purpose of providing an environment in which the creativity of its individual stars can be maximised.

- Mentor models most likely to thrive in person cultures: colleague, consultant, developer of talent, facilitator, opener of doors, coach.
- Mentor models least likely to succeed in person cultures: assessor, appraiser, discipliner instructor, leader.

### *Activity 12*

- Do you recognise any of the organisation cultures above as relating to your own organisation?
- Using the organisational features below, describe your organisation to someone who has had no experience of it.
  - Major purpose of the organisation
  - Size of organisation
  - Organisational structure
  - New or established
  - Buildings/plant/accommodation
  - Type of organisation – private, public, not-for-profit, voluntary, charity, co-operative, partnership, small and medium-sized enterprise (SME)
  - The people who work in the organisation
  - How they work – individually, in teams
  - The range of specialisms or expertise represented
  - Organisational culture
- Looking back at your preferred models of mentoring identified in Section 3.1, do you think they will be appropriate in your organisation as described above?

## The role of the mentor in apprentice training structures

*The Richard Review of Apprenticeships* emphasised the importance of mentoring in the New Apprenticeships:

> *The Government should consider specifying that the employer and apprentice come together at the beginning of the apprenticeship and sign an agreement,*

*setting out what is expected of them. This could include an explicit commitment to work towards the relevant apprenticeship qualification. It should also spell out the training that will be delivered, by whom and where, and the time off work allowed for this. It should be clear who is available to mentor and support the apprentice – in the training organisation and the firm. This is simply good practice, and happens in some cases today. But, going forward, it needs to be a routine part of the approach.*
(Richard, 2012, p 94)

The number of partners in training and their relationship with the apprentice and each other is more complex in the New Apprenticeship structure. Education and Skills Funding Agency guidance for employers on funding (ESFA, 2018) illustrates this. The 'employer' is the organisation that has a contract of service and an apprenticeship agreement with an apprentice. The 'employer-provider' can deliver some, or all, of the 'off-the-job' training element of an apprenticeship to their own staff. The 'main (training) provider' will have the overall responsibility for the training and on-programme assessment conducted by themselves and their 'delivery subcontractors'. A 'provider' will be any organisation on the register of apprenticeship training providers contracted through a main provider for the delivery of training and on-programme assessment, as part of the employer's agreed apprenticeship programme. This includes companies, charities, bodies, colleges, universities, sole traders, and other types of legal entity, including those who are in the same group as, or are associated with, the main provider. Although most likely to be a fellow employee of the apprentice, it is possible that you may be a member of the training provider organisation or its associates. Indeed, any one apprentice may have more than one mentor in the different organisations supporting their apprenticeship. Furthermore, because of this complexity and the varied patterns of off-the-job and on-the-job training, it is possible that you will, as well as mentor, be acting in other roles with them – such as trainer for your employer.

### *Activity 13*

- With your apprentice, discuss the particular training structure that supports them during their apprenticeship. The complexity of this structure means that the effective liaison between the mentor and those in other roles to monitor the progress of apprentices may be challenging.

## Successful communication between the mentor and key parties

Some of the key parties involved in the apprenticeship are: apprentice, peer colleague in same company, manager in same company, supervisor in same company, off-the-job training provider such as FE college or private training provider, other mentors within and outside company, end-point assessor. Consider which features would tend to aid successful communication between the mentor and these key parties and which features might challenge successful communication. Table 3e provides you with some ideas.

*Table 3e Communication aids and challenges*

| Communication between mentor and... | Features tending to aid successful communication | Features tending to challenge successful communication |
|---|---|---|
| Apprentice | • Where there is a close working relationship, eg one carpenter + apprentice<br>• Where mentor can field queries from apprentice they might not want to take to manager/supervisor<br>• Where mentor is non-threatening, such as a peer mentor<br>• Where mentor can act as a buffer/conduit between apprentice and manager<br>Others? | • Where mentor has more than one role, eg, as supervisor with different role and responsibilities from mentor role<br>• Where mentor and apprentice are in different departments<br>Others? |
| Peer colleague in same company | • Where mentor has networked or advocated on apprentice's behalf<br>Others? | • Where they have differing views about how apprentice learns<br>• If mentor v peer colleague is unrealistic about apprentice's progress<br>Others? |
| Manager in same company | • Where the mentor is a respected member of staff<br>Others? | • Where management does not fully back the mentor scheme and feel the costs outweigh the benefits<br>Others? |
| Supervisor in same company | • Where they share the company culture<br>Others? | • Where the supervisor is more concerned with performance management of apprentice than with their progress in learning<br>Others? |
| Off-the-job training provider such as FE college or private training provider | • Where mentor is able to ensure there is a three-way relationship by sitting in on meetings, for example<br>Others? | • Where workloads, transport, lack of technology create barriers to liaison<br>Others? |
| Other mentors within and outside company | • Where mentors see team mentoring as an opportunity to extend collegiality<br>Others? | Others? |

*(continued)*

| Communication between mentor and... | Features tending to aid successful communication | Features tending to challenge successful communication |
|---|---|---|
| End-point assessor | • Established channels of communication between mentor and EPA<br><br>Others? | • Where extensive working with apprentice threatens mentor's objectivity in assessment<br><br>Others? |
| Other parties? | | |

## 3.9 MAINTAINING YOUR OCCUPATIONAL CURRENCY AND ENSURING CONTINUOUS PROFESSIONAL DEVELOPMENT

We saw earlier that one of the key elements in building respect on the part of a mentee for a mentor was the mentor's own high quality of professional/occupational practice. It is important, therefore, that you engage in activities that will ensure you maintain this level of practice so that you can model this for the apprentice. The kinds of activities available to you will depend on your own professional/occupational role and the opportunities both within and outside your organisation. Below are professional/occupational development activities that may be available to you.

- Observations of your practice – by colleagues, managers, staff developers.
- Appraisals.
- Mentoring.
- Involvement in subject/skills area network meetings.
- Training in emerging technologies.
- Conference attendance.
- Organisation staff development days.
- Action learning sets (a group of work-based colleagues who meet regularly – at each, one presents a work-related problem and the others, guided by a facilitator, discuss and analyse this problem).
- Recording experiences, meetings, professional activities, thoughts/ideas.
- Professional/occupational updating.
- Learning visit to industry/commercial organisation, public services.
- Secondment.
- Updating knowledge through TV, internet, social media.
- Short courses.

- Consultancy.
- Research projects.
- Gaining literacy, numeracy and English for speakers of other languages (ESOL) qualifications.
- Shadowing.
- Awarding organisation subject-specific updating.
- Taking on examiner, verifier or assessor responsibilities.
- Organising trips, residentials and work placements.

### *Activity 14*

- Have you completed any of the above activities in the last six months?
- Are there other activities you have engaged in that are not specified?
- Are you intending to engage in any development activities in the next six months? If so, specify them in Your action plan 3 in Section 3.10.

## 3.10 YOUR ACTION PLAN 3

### *Activity 15*

- Complete the action plan below based on the activities in this chapter. Table 3f is available electronically at www.criticalpublishing.com/the-new-apprenticeships.

*Table 3f Your action plan 3*

| **Issue** | **Proposed actions** | **Responsibility for actions** | **Intended targets/ outcomes** | **Timing** |
|---|---|---|---|---|
| 3.1 Mentoring roles and models | Eg, reconsider the roles I have with my mentee | Myself and mentee | Broaden strategies I need to use if necessary | Immediate |
| 3.2 Learning from experience and reflective practice | Eg, develop a means by which mentee's reflection is accurately recorded | Myself, training partners, awarding organisations | Recording of reflection leads to improvement in performance | Next six months |

| | | | | |
|---|---|---|---|---|
| 3.3 The mentoring cycle | Eg, schedule a mentoring cycle with mentee | Myself and mentee | Develop a cycle that builds mentees' learning | Next six months |
| 3.4 Recording learner progress | Eg, develop a means by which mentee's progress is accurately recorded | Myself, training partners, awarding organisations, end-point assessment organisations | Mentee's progress is easily monitored by all parties | Next six months |
| 3.5 Managing and maintaining the mentor–mentee relationship | Eg, evaluate own management of my relationship with mentee | Myself and mentee | Adjust any aspects of management of relationship accordingly | Next six months |
| 3.6 Mentoring and coaching | Eg, develop own questioning skills | Myself | Investigation of coaching literature<br>Approach staff training/HR for guidance on coaching training | Immediate |
| 3.7 Safety, health and the environment | Eg, investigate HSE requirements of apprenticeship standards and end-point assessment | Myself, training partners, awarding organisations, end-point assessment organisations | Familiarisation with apprenticeship standards and assessment plan | Immediate |
| 3.8 Your organisation and your partners in training | Eg, familiarise yourself with other partners in supporting the apprenticeship and their roles | Myself and partners | Meetings, company literature, web search | Immediate |
| 3.9 Maintaining your occupational currency and ensuring continuous professional development | Eg, organisation staff development days<br>Short course<br>Learning visit to industry/ commercial organisation, public services | Myself and colleagues | Maintaining my occupational currency and ensuring continuous professional development | Ongoing |

# 4 Mentoring and coaching skills

**CHAPTER CONTENT**

This chapter covers:



## 4.1 MODELS OF MENTORING AND COACHING

### Models of mentoring

At the beginning of Chapter 3, three continua for the key features or dimensions of what kind of mentor you are were identified (Klasen and Clutterbuck, 2002).

- The first is the directive/non-directive continuum. This indicates the extent to which you tell/instruct/show your mentee what to do, rather than leave the initiative to them. So directive roles would be 'teacher' and 'instructor', with less directive roles being 'helper', 'opener of doors'.
- Second, there is the cognitive/emotional continuum. Do you see yourself as conveying knowledge/information as an 'expert', rather than attending to the more emotional dimensions of your mentee's development as 'counsellor' or 'friend'?
- Finally, do you see your roles as mainly active, as a 'discipliner' or 'assessor' rather acting more passively as 'colleague' or 'facilitator'?

You were then asked to plot your position on each of these three continua.

Directive ........................................ Non-directive
Cognitive ........................................ Emotional
Active ........................................ Passive

Now revisit the first row of your action plan from Activity 15 in Chapter 3.

*Table 4a Your action plan 3 revisited*

| Issue | Proposed actions | Responsibility for actions | Intended targets/ outcomes | Timing |
|---|---|---|---|---|
| 3.1 Mentoring roles and models | Eg, reconsider the roles I have with my mentee | Myself and mentee | Broaden strategies I need to use if necessary | Immediate |

### *Activity 1*

- Consider the proposed actions you intend to take regarding the mentoring roles and models you will be adopting with your apprentice. What was it that gave rise to these changes?

## Models of coaching

There is a range of coaching models that you may or may not be familiar with. Solutions-focused coaching encourages the coachee to solve problems in order to build on their strengths and hit their targets. Values-based approaches stress the importance of identifying the coachee's values as key to their own development, while directive and non-directive coaching vary in the degree of input and action there is from the coach and coachee respectively. Content-focused approaches are often used with teachers to improve their teaching via a deeper understanding of their subject knowledge. One of the most popular approaches is goal-focused coaching and one of the best-known and most widely used of these is the GROW model developed by Sir John Whitmore and colleagues (Whitmore, 2017). GROW stands for the four distinct stages of coaching.

1. ***G****oal setting for the session as well as the short and long term*
2. ***R****eality checking to explore the current situation*
3. ***O****ptions and alternative strategies or courses of action*
4. ***W****hat is to be done, When, by Whom, and the Will to do it.*

(Whitmore, 2017, p 96)

For Whitmore, the key to using this model successfully is:

> *first to spend sufficient time exploring 'G' until the coachee sets a goal which is both inspirational and stretching for them, and then to move flexibly through the sequence according to your intuition, including revisiting the goal if needed.*
>
> *STEP 1: WHAT ARE YOUR GOALS?*
>
> - *Identifies and clarifies the type of goal through an understanding of ultimate goals, performance goals and progress goals along the way.*
> - *Provides understanding of principal aims and aspirations.*
> - *Clarifies the desired result from the session.*
>
> *STEP 2: WHAT IS THE REALITY?*
>
> - *Assesses the current situation in terms of the action taken so far.*
> - *Clarifies the results and effects of previously taken actions.*
> - *Provides understanding of internal obstacles and blocks currently preventing or limiting progression.*
>
> *STEP 3: WHAT ARE YOUR OPTIONS?*
>
> - *Identifies the possibilities and alternatives.*
> - *Outlines and questions a number of strategies for progression.*
>
> *STEP 4: WHAT WILL YOU DO?*
>
> - *Provides understanding of what has been learned and what can be changed to achieve the initial goals.*
> - *Creates a summary and plan of action for implementation of the identified steps.*
> - *Outlines possible future obstacles.*
> - *Considers the continued achievement of the goals, and the support and development that may be required.*
> - *Estimates the certainty of commitment to the agreed actions.*
> - *Highlights how accountability and achievement of the goals will be ensured.*
>
> (Whitmore, 2017, p 100)

## *Activity 2*

- On the Institute for Apprenticeship's website (www.instituteforapprenticeships.org/apprenticeship-standards) locate the approved standard that is the closest to your apprenticeship as you were asked to do in Activity 6 in Chapter 1 and Activity 6 in Chapter 2. Select two or three closely allied skills and for each, start '*exploring "G" until the coachee sets a goal which is both inspirational and stretching for them*'.

Some of the questions which may help in this process are suggested by Whitmore.

- *What would be an inspirational goal for you?*
- *What outcome are you looking for?*
- *What will it bring you personally?*
- *How would you break this goal down into smaller pieces?*
- *What milestones can you identify? What are their timeframes?*
- *Imagine three months from now, all obstacles are removed, and you have achieved your goal:*
    - *What do you see/hear/feel?*
    - *What does it look like?*
    - *What are people saying to you?*
    - *How does it feel? What new elements are in place?*
    - *What is different?*

(Whitmore, 2017, pp 257–8)

## 4.2 EMOTIONAL INTELLIGENCE

You saw in Chapter 2 that Daniel Goleman identified five social and emotional competencies.

1. Self-awareness – understand one's emotions, strengths and weaknesses, and recognise their impact on others.
2. Self-regulation – manage one's feelings and adapt to changing circumstances.
3. Social skills – manage others' feelings well.
4. Empathy – recognise, understand, and consider other people's feelings.
5. Motivation – using your feelings to achieve your goals.

These are some of the 'soft skills' that are central to effective mentoring and coaching. They are also likely to be important as skills and behaviours required in your apprentice's occupational role.

## Activity 3

- In Table 4b, where 1 is high, self-assess your own emotional competencies against each bullet point.
- Ask your apprentice to assess his or her own emotional competencies.

*Table 4b Competency framework*

| Personal competence | | 1 | 2 | 3 | 4 | 5 |
|---|---|---|---|---|---|---|
| | **SELF-AWARENESS** | | | | | |
| **Emotional awareness: recognising one's emotions and their effects** | People with this competence:<br>• know which emotions they are feeling and why<br>• realise the links between their feelings and what they think, do, and say<br>• recognise how their feelings affect their performance<br>• have a guiding awareness of their values and goals | | | | | |
| **Accurate self-assessment: knowing one's strengths and limits** | People with this competence are:<br>• aware of their strengths and weaknesses<br>• reflective, learning from experience<br>• open to candid feedback, new perspectives, continuous learning, and self-development<br>• able to show a sense of humour and perspective about themselves | | | | | |
| **Self-confidence: sureness about one's self-worth and capabilities** | People with this competence:<br>• present themselves with self-assurance; have presence<br>• can voice views that are unpopular and go out on a limb for what is right<br>• are decisive, able to make sound decisions despite uncertainties and pressures | | | | | |
| | **SELF-REGULATION** | | | | | |
| **Self-control: managing disruptive emotions and impulses** | People with this competence:<br>• manage their impulsive feelings and distressing emotions well<br>• stay composed, positive, and unflappable even in trying moments<br>• think clearly and stay focused under pressure | | | | | |

| | | |
|---|---|---|
| **Trustworthiness: maintaining standards of honesty and integrity** | People with this competence:<br>• act ethically and are above reproach<br>• build trust through their reliability and authenticity<br>• admit their own mistakes and confront unethical actions in others<br>• take tough, principled stands even if they are unpopular | |
| **Conscientiousness: taking responsibility for personal performance** | People with this competence:<br>• meet commitments and keep promises<br>• hold themselves accountable for meeting their objectives<br>• are organised and careful in their work | |
| **Adaptability: flexibility in handling change** | People with this competence:<br>• smoothly handle multiple demands, shifting priorities and rapid change<br>• adapt their responses and tactics to fit fluid circumstances<br>• are flexible in how they see events | |
| **Innovativeness: being comfortable with and open to novel ideas and new information** | People with this competence:<br>• seek out fresh ideas from a wide variety of sources<br>• entertain original solutions to problems<br>• generate new ideas<br>• take fresh perspectives and risks in their thinking | |
| | **SELF-MOTIVATION** | |
| **Achievement drive: striving to improve or meet a standard of excellence** | People with this competence:<br>• are results-oriented, with a high drive to meet their objectives and standards<br>• set challenging goals and take calculated risks<br>• pursue information to reduce uncertainty and find ways to do better<br>• learn how to improve their performance | |
| **Commitment: aligning with the goals of the group or organisation** | People with this competence:<br>• readily make personal or group sacrifices to meet a larger organisational goal<br>• find a sense of purpose in the larger mission | |

| Personal competence | | 1 2 3 4 5 |
|---|---|---|
| | • use the group's core values in making decisions and clarifying choices<br>• actively seek out opportunities to fulfil the group's mission | |
| **Initiative: readiness to act on opportunities** | People with this competence:<br>• are ready to seize opportunities<br>• pursue goals beyond what's required or expected of them<br>• cut through red tape and bend the rules when necessary to get the job done<br>• mobilise others through unusual, enterprising efforts | |
| **Optimism: persistence in pursuing goals despite obstacles and setbacks** | People with this competence:<br>• persist in seeking goals despite obstacles and setbacks<br>• operate from hope of success rather than fear of failure<br>• see setbacks as due to manageable circumstance rather than a personal flaw | |
| | **SOCIAL AWARENESS** | |
| **Empathy: sensing others' feelings and perspective, and taking an active interest in their concerns** | People with this competence:<br>• are attentive to emotional cues and listen well<br>• show sensitivity and understand others' perspectives<br>• help out based on understanding other people's needs and feelings | |
| **Service orientation: anticipating, recognising and meeting customers' needs** | People with this competence:<br>• understand customers' needs and match them to services or products<br>• seek ways to increase customers' satisfaction and loyalty<br>• gladly offer appropriate assistance<br>• grasp a customer's perspective, acting as a trusted adviser | |
| **Developing others: sensing what others need in order to develop, and bolstering their abilities** | People with this competence:<br>• acknowledge and reward people's strengths, accomplishments, and development<br>• offer useful feedback and identify people's needs for development | |

| | | |
|---|---|---|
| | • mentor, give timely coaching and offer assignments that challenge and grow a person's skills | |
| **Leveraging diversity: cultivating opportunities through diverse people** | People with this competence:<br>• respect and relate well to people from varied backgrounds<br>• understand diverse worldviews and are sensitive to group differences<br>• see diversity as opportunity, creating an environment where diverse people can thrive<br>• challenge bias and intolerance | |
| **Political awareness: reading a group's emotional currents and power relationships** | People with this competence:<br>• accurately read key power relationships<br>• detect crucial social networks<br>• understand the forces that shape views and actions of clients, customers, or competitors<br>• accurately read situations and organisational and external realities | |
| | **SOCIAL SKILLS** | |
| **Influence: wielding effective tactics for persuasion** | People with this competence:<br>• are skilled at persuasion<br>• fine-tune presentations to appeal to the listener<br>• use complex strategies like indirect influence to build consensus and support<br>• orchestrate dramatic events to effectively make a point | |
| **Communication: sending clear and convincing messages** | People with this competence:<br>• are effective in give-and-take, registering emotional cues in attuning their message<br>• deal with difficult issues straightforwardly<br>• listen well, seek mutual understanding, and welcome sharing of information fully<br>• foster open communication and stay receptive to bad news as well as good | |

| Personal competence | | 1 2 3 4 5 |
|---|---|---|
| **Leadership: inspiring and guiding groups and people** | People with this competence:<br>• articulate and arouse enthusiasm for a shared vision and mission<br>• step forward to lead as needed, regardless of position<br>• guide the performance of others while holding them accountable<br>• lead by example | |
| **Change catalyst: initiating or managing change** | People with this competence:<br>• recognise the need for change and remove barriers<br>• challenge the status quo to acknowledge the need for change<br>• champion the change and enlist others in its pursuit<br>• model the change expected of others | |
| **Conflict management: negotiating and resolving disagreements** | People with this competence:<br>• handle difficult people and tense situations with diplomacy and tact<br>• spot potential conflict, bring disagreements into the open and help de-escalate<br>• encourage debate and open discussion<br>• orchestrate win–win solutions | |
| **Building bonds: nurturing instrumental relationships** | People with this competence:<br>• cultivate and maintain extensive informal networks<br>• seek out relationships that are mutually beneficial<br>• build rapport and keep others in the loop<br>• make and maintain personal friendships among work associates | |
| **Collaboration and co-operation: working with others toward shared goals** | People with this competence:<br>• balance a focus on task with attention to relationships<br>• collaborate, sharing plans, information and resources<br>• promote a friendly, co-operative climate<br>• spot and nurture opportunities for collaboration | |

| | | |
|---|---|---|
| **Team capabilities: creating group synergy in pursuing collective goals** | People with this competence:<br>• model team qualities like respect, helpfulness and co-operation<br>• draw all members into active and enthusiastic participation<br>• build team identity, esprit de corps and commitment<br>• protect the group and its reputation; share credit | |

Adapted from General Competence Framework of Consortium for Research on Emotional Intelligence in Organizations (1998)

### *Activity 4*

- Both you and your apprentice should focus on the competencies for which you scored 3, 4 or 5 in Activity 3. Are these emotional competencies you feel you need for your mentoring or in your apprentice's occupational role?
- If so, how are you intending to develop these? Complete row 4.2 in 'Your action plan 4' at the end of this chapter.

## 4.3 BUILDING RAPPORT, TRUST AND RESPECT

At the beginning of his Chapter 3, 'Coaching is emotional intelligence in practice', Whitmore suggest carrying out the following exercise.

### *Activity 5*

- *Recall someone you loved being with when you were younger – not a parent, but perhaps a grandparent, a teacher or a role model. When you were with this person:*
  1. *What did they do that you liked so much?*
  2. *How did you feel?*
- *Think about the person's attitudes and behaviours. Write down your answers.*

(Whitmore, 2017, p 40)

- Now please carry out the exercise for yourself.

Whitman and his colleagues found that people everywhere had broadly the same response to these questions, irrespective of country or culture:

| **The person...** | **I felt...** |
|---|---|
| listened to me | special |
| believed in me | valued |
| challenged me | confident |
| trusted and respected me | safe, cared for |
| gave me time and full attention | supported |
| trusted me as equal | fun, enthusiasm |
| | self-belief |

The qualities listed in Activity 5 are, of course, some of the key qualities and outcomes we saw in Section 3.5 as necessary for managing and maintaining the mentor–mentee relationship. And it might be an interesting exercise to imagine what you think *your* apprentice will say about *you* in the years to come regarding what you did that they liked so much and how they felt about it.

## *Activity 6*

- Revisit the emotional competency framework in Section 4.2. Select those personal competencies you feel are important in the development of rapport with, trust of and respect for you on the part of your apprentice.
- Now, create a pyramid of the six competencies you feel are most important to you and rank them as below, the most important at the top.

There is no correct arrangement of key competencies: yours will reflect your own view of your role and the context of the mentor–mentee relationship. One mentor created the pyramid in Figure 4a as a result of this exercise.

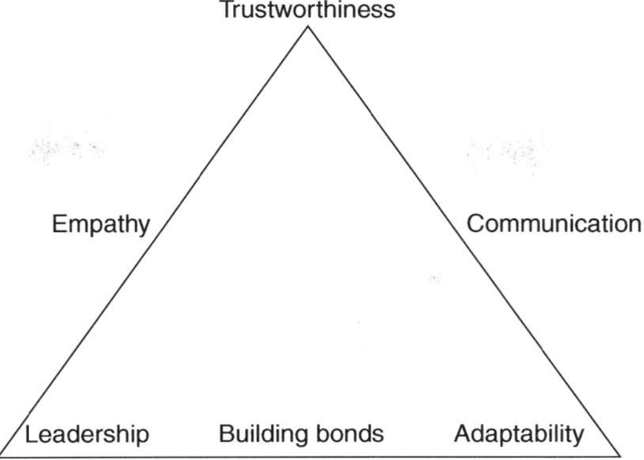


Figure 4a Competencies pyramid

This mentor explained that he thought trustworthiness was the bedrock of his relationship with his apprentice and that without it, no effective relationship was possible. He felt his apprentice needed reliable and consistent support and the belief in him to be professional and keep confidences. He felt he needed to be a good listener and understand the apprentice and his perspective. Also important was the ability to give clear messages and instructions. He felt he needed to lead by example and be a professional role model. He felt he needed to demonstrate how to form and maintain good relationships with work colleagues. And he thought he should demonstrate adaptability and flexibility in his relationship with his apprenticeship.

Could you now provide a rationale or explanation for the arrangement of the personal competencies in your pyramid?

## 4.4 QUESTIONING

### Framing questions

To obtain the answer or response you want, you will need to frame your question carefully. Below is a series of contexts in which questions are asked and the purposes for which they were asked.

#### *Activity 7*

- For each question in Table 4c, evaluate how effective it is given the context and purpose.

*Table 4c Contexts, purposes and questions*

| **Context** | **Purpose** | **Question** |
|---|---|---|
| The apprentice is late and the mentor wants to know why. | The mentor needs a reason to note in the apprentice's record. | 'What time d'you call this?' |
| A construction mentor and her apprentice are fixing brackets to a wall. | To test the apprentice's awareness about which rawl plugs are suitable for different surfaces and walls. | 'So we have a cavity wall here. Is this the right rawl plug for it?' |
| A retail mentor is in a simulated work environment with his apprentice. | To test the apprentice's knowledge of the appropriate documentation for retail tasks. | 'And I would use Form G for a refund, yes?' |
| A construction mentor and her apprentice are fixing brackets to a wall. | To test the apprentice's practical skill in using a drill. | 'So, this drill – tell me about how you would use it.' |
| A trainer is in a simulated aircraft cabin with an apprentice. | To discover the trainee's full knowledge and understanding regarding passenger safety in the cabin. | 'So what's important about safety in the cabin?' |
| A painter/decorator mentor is with an apprentice on site. | To bring to the apprentice's attention the results of using differing application methods for paint. | 'Oi – [pointing at wall the apprentice has just painted] what d'you call that?' |
| A police trainer asks a trainee to define the law on breach of the peace. She gives the following definition: '*Disturbing the peace is a crime generally defined as the unsettling of proper order in a public space through one's actions. This can include creating loud noise by fighting or challenging to fight, disturbing others by loud and unreasonable noise (including loud music), or using profanity*' (Wikipedia, 2018). | The trainer wants to know if the trainee is aware that in some jurisdictions, the law is framed in a vague way, which can make its violation difficult to prove. | 'So what's problematic about it?' |
| A retail mentor is in a simulated work environment with her apprentice. | The mentor wants to find out how the apprentice would deal with a customer who was rude to them. | 'So imagine a customer is rude to you. What would you do?' |
| The construction apprentice is now attempting to determine how level the shelf is with a spirit level. | The mentor wants to inform the apprentice about proper practice with a spirit level. | 'That's not the way to do it, is it?' |

- The question 'What time d'you call this?' is not an attempt to ascertain whether the apprentice is capable of telling the time, nor a really a request for reasons why the apprentice is late, but more an admonishment for being late. This is telling off disguised as a question. People often find it easier to express feelings or emotions indirectly because they either are afraid of expressing them directly or do not know how to.
- Closed questions are those that are only capable of a yes/no answer. So the construction mentor is only going to get yes or no in answer to her question rather than testing the apprentice's awareness about which rawl plugs are suitable for different surfaces and walls.
- The retail mentor asks a leading question 'And I would use Form G for a refund, yes?' of the apprentice, which suggests she wants the answer 'Yes'; or it's a trick question with her pretending to favour one form while another is appropriate – neither of which is a fair test of the apprentice's knowledge.
- 'So, this drill – tell me about how you would use it' is an open question. These are usually designed to give the responder full and creative capacity to respond not, as is the case here, to test the apprentice's practical skill in using a drill.
- 'So what's important about safety in the cabin?' is a very general or ambiguous question when it is passenger safety the trainer is concerned with.
- 'Oi – [pointing at wall the apprentice has just painted] what d'you call that?' is insulting and offensive whatever the relationship between mentor and mentee, and is unlikely to successfully bring to the apprentice's attention the results of using differing application methods for paint.
- The police trainer's question 'So what's problematic about it?' is a follow-up or probing question and these need to be more specific and focused than the original question.
- It's difficult to see how the apprentice might respond to 'So imagine a customer is rude to you. What would you do?' and the situation would be one where a role play or simulation would be more appropriate than a question.
- 'That's not the way to do it, is it?' Humiliation is never an appropriate preparation for informing a learner about proper practice.

## Generating questions using Bloom's Taxonomy

Bloom classified educational objectives into three domains: the cognitive domain in which objectives were related to knowledge and understanding; the affective domain, which contained those objectives relating to attitudes, emotions and feelings; and the psycho-motor domain in which the objectives related to practical, physical skills (Bloom et al, 1956). Below are verbs that describe activities relating to objectives in the cognitive domain. Generating questions relating to these activity verbs allows you to ensure your questions are likely to invite answers demonstrating different types of cognitive activity.

*Table 4d Questions for cognitive activities*

| **Activity verbs** | **Remembering** | **Understanding** | **Applying** | **Analysing** | **Evaluating** | **Creating** |
|---|---|---|---|---|---|---|
| Questions | What happened after...?<br><br>How many...?<br><br>Who was it that...?<br><br>Can you name the...?<br><br>Describe what happened at...<br><br>Who spoke to...?<br><br>Can you tell why...?<br><br>Find the meaning of...<br><br>What is...?<br><br>Which is true or false...? | Can you write in your own words...?<br><br>Can you write a brief outline...?<br><br>What do you think could have happened next...?<br><br>Who do you think...?<br><br>What was the main idea...?<br><br>Can you distinguish between...?<br><br>What differences exist between...?<br><br>Can you provide an example of what you mean...?<br><br>Can you provide a definition for...? | Do you know another instance where...?<br><br>Could this have happened in...?<br><br>Can you group by characteristics such as...?<br><br>What factors would you change if...?<br><br>Can you apply the method used to some experience of your own...?<br><br>What questions would you ask of...?<br><br>From the information given, can you develop a set of instructions about...?<br><br>Would this information be useful if you had...? | If ... happened, what might the ending have been?<br><br>How was this similar to...?<br><br>What was the underlying theme of...?<br><br>What do you see as other possible outcomes?<br><br>Why did ... changes occur?<br><br>Can you compare your ... with that presented in...?<br><br>Can you explain what must have happened when...?<br><br>What are some of the problems of...?<br><br>Can you distinguish between...?<br><br>What were some of the motives behind...?<br><br>What was the turning point in the game?<br><br>What was the problem with...? | Is there a better solution to...?<br><br>Judge the value of...<br><br>Can you defend your position about...?<br><br>Do you think ... is a good or a bad thing?<br><br>How would you have handled...?<br><br>What changes to ... would you recommend?<br><br>Do you believe ...?<br><br>How would you feel if...?<br><br>How effective are...?<br><br>What do you think about...? | Can you design a ... to ...?<br><br>Can you see a possible solution to...?<br><br>If you had access to all resources how would you deal with...?<br><br>Why don't you devise your own way to deal with...?<br><br>What would happen if...?<br><br>How many ways can you...?<br><br>Can you create new and unusual uses for...?<br><br>Can you develop a proposal which would...? |

Adapted from table at Wikispaces (2018b)

## Questions for purposes

Specific questions are designed to elicit the coachee's goals for a specific discussion or for the coaching experience overall. For Whitmore, they would be used at the first stage of the GROW model.

- *What outcome are you looking for?*
- *What will it bring you personally?*
- *What would it mean to you to achieve this?*
- *When do you need to have achieved this outcome?*

(Whitmore, 2017, pp 257–8)

Pemberton and Cray call these '*Questions to unearth outcomes*':

- *What would you like to focus on today?*
- *How can this conversation be most helpful to you?*
- *What's missing?*
- *What do you want to leave behind as your legacy when you move into your next role?*

(Pemberton and Cray, 2013, p 19)

Questions exploring current realities would be used at the second stage of the GROW model:

- *What is happening at the moment?*
- *How important is this to you?*
- *On a scale of 1–10, if an ideal situation is 10, what number are you at now?*
- *How do you feel about this?*

(Whitmore, 2017, p 258)

Pemberton calls these '*What*' questions:

- *What are you most worried about?*
- *What do you need to do right now?*
- *What are the risks in this?*
- *What decisions do you have to make?*

(Pemberton, 2013)

At the third and fourth stages of the GROW model, the '*options*' and '*will*' stages, Whitmore would use the following types of questions:

- *What could you do?*
- *What ideas do you have?*

- *What steps could you take?*
- *What else could you do?*
- *What will you do?*
- *How will you do that?*
- *When will you do it?*
- *Who will you talk to?*

(Whitmore, 2017, pp 259–60)

Pemberton and Cray call these '*Questions to find solutions*' and '*Questions to move things forward*':

- *If you had all the time/money/skill you needed to deal – what would you do?*
- *What one thing can you do that will make a difference to...?*
- *What does your intuition tell you?*
- *What does good enough look like?*
- *What are you going to do about this in the next 24 hours?*
- *What can you do in the next week/month?*
- *What would move your commitment/confidence to 10?*
- *What would be the first sign that the change is happening?*

(Pemberton and Cray, 2013, pp 19–20)

## Scenario

### Cabin crew coaching conversation

Dean is a level 3 cabin crew apprentice and is having some problems with spoken skills related to this role. He comes to you for some additional coaching in this area.

### Pre-observation conversation

**Mentor:** *OK Dean – what do you want to focus on today?*

**Dean:** *Apparently there were problems getting what I was saying when I was using the intercom. And I had to repeat myself a number of times when I was talking to the passenger role players.*

**Mentor:** *So people aren't clear what you're saying to them?*

**Dean:** *Apparently...*

**Mentor:** *Why 'apparently'?*

**Dean:** *Well, because no-one's actually said what it is they can't understand or why they can't understand it.*

**Mentor:** *So what do you want to do about it?*

**Dean:** *I thought you might have a few ideas!*

**Mentor:** *No – I mean, how will you know if you've improved these skills?*

**Dean:** *I s'pose when I don't get these responses that people don't understand me but, before that, I probably need to understand where I'm going wrong.*

**Mentor:** *And so do I if I'm going to help you.*

**Dean:** *So I need to get some feedback – feedback I haven't had so far?*

**Mentor:** *Exactly.*

The mentor suspects, although she hasn't said this, that Dean is inhibited in a formal training session with other colleagues and role players looking on so arranges some one-to-one sessions in the cabin simulator when Dean can both make intercom announcements and interact with the mentor in some of the standard crew–passenger exchanges.

## Post-observation conversation

**Mentor:** *So, did you think you did worse, as well or better in the sessions with me than in the training sessions?*

**Dean:** *Better, definitely. It's much easier when my mates aren't there. Or people role-playing.*

**Mentor:** *But you're going to have to operate in a real, live situation at some point, aren't you? What could you do to keep on improving?*

**Dean:** *Practise?*

**Mentor:** *Exactly – you might want to video yourself on your tablet. Or ask your friends or family to listen to you.*

**Dean:** *OK...*

**Mentor:** *But you need to know what to look out for and be aware of.*

**Dean:** *Like?*

**Mentor:** *OK – so, first, do you know what stress is?*

**Dean:** *Tell me about it – every time I have to make an announcement!*

**Mentor:** *Not that kind of stress – stress in speech.*

**Dean:** *OK.*

**Mentor:** *Now a syllable is a bit or part of a word. How many parts has the word 'syllable'?*

**Dean:** *Syll-a-ble – three.*

**Mentor:** *And in words of more than one syllable, one of the syllables will take a natural stress or emphasis. So in 'punctual'?*

**Dean:** *On 'punct'?*

**Mentor:** *Yes – 'Important'?*

**Dean:** *On 'por'.*

**Mentor:** *Exactly. Now sometimes, you may need to exaggerate the natural stress of a word to signal you want to draw attention to it. 'What I'm about to tell you is very imPORtant.'*

[The mentor goes on to explain other relevant aspects of speech – articulation, tone, volume, pace.]

**Mentor:** *So when do you think you'll be able to demonstrate marked improvement?*

**Dean:** *Can you give me a fortnight?*

**Mentor:** *Another observation two weeks today, then?*

### *Activity 8*

- How effective was the mentor's questioning?
- Were there any points where he realised a question hadn't worked and quickly asked another?
- Although the emphasis in coaching is on the coachee developing *themselves*, sometimes, some teaching/tutoring may be necessary as part of the coaching conversation (see Section 4.7). At which point was this necessary in the conversation above?

## 4.5 ACTIVE LISTENING

When we think about listening, it is easy to fall into the trap of conceiving of this as a passive role, the receive side of a transmission–reception model. But we know that human interaction is richer, more complex and dynamic than this. The speaker is affected in what and how they say it by the listener's activities: how the listener is responding, whether the listener appears to be understanding what they are saying, the feedback the listener is giving through what they say or through their body language or non-verbal communication (NVC). So the listener has a very active role in the conversation and when we refer to this as done well, we call it 'active listening'. Furthermore, active listening requires the listener to be interpreting, structuring and organising what they hear as they are going along.

## Activity 9

- Watch a TV news broadcast, which you should record, noting down the key items so that you are able to convey these to a third party. After the broadcast, convey these items to a third party. Now you and the third party should watch the recorded news broadcast and make a judgement about how accurate and how full your summary was.

## Activity 10

- Interview your apprentice for a videoed item in a programme about the value of apprenticeships. You might want to write down some prompt questions in advance but be prepared to ask different questions according to how the apprentice responds. Ask a third party to video this on a tablet. The three of you should review the recording and make a judgement about how effective a listener you were.

Some of the issues that might affect your judgement are:

- whether the interviewer interrupted the speaker unnecessarily (for example, not anticipating the speaker was going to go on to address the interrupting question anyway);
- the interviewer jumping to conclusions about what the speaker was going to say – sentence completion;
- the interviewer concentrating on notes or the next question as the speaker was speaking;
- the interviewer not maintaining eye contact;
- the interviewer being unaware they were making distracting gestures.

Carole Pemberton (2013) suggests that as mentors we should listen to not only what we are hearing but perhaps what we're not hearing as well. So active listening on the basis of what we are hearing leads us to encourage ('*tell me more...*'), clarify ('*can I just check...?*'), summarise ('*so what you are telling me is...*'), and empathise ('I understand how difficult...'). This, Pemberton calls '*listening above the water*'. However, although we might not directly observe this, we may sense, suspect or intuit that the mentee has certain beliefs, emotions, agendas and values driving them, and ascertaining what these are. Pemberton calls '*listening below the water*'.

Whitmore summarises active listening skills as follows:

- *reflecting/mirroring – saying someone's exact words back to them;*
- *paraphrasing – using slightly different word(s) which do not change the substance or meaning of what the other person has said;*
- *summarising – repeating back what has been said but more briefly, without changing the substance or meaning;*
- *clarifying – expressing succinctly the essence/core of what has been said and adding something valuable picked up intuitively from emotions or discrepancies in words or expressions of face or body that haven't been said in words, to generate insight and clarity for the speaker and check that you understood: 'It sounds like...What would you say?';*
- *encouraging self-expression – building trust and intimacy to encourage openness;*
- *suspending judgement, criticism and attachment – keeping an open mind. Judgements and criticisms make people defensive and stop them from talking;*
- *listening for potential – focusing on capabilities and strengths, not past performance or seeing someone as a problem. What could the person unleash if there were no limits?*
- *listening with heart – listening to non-verbal messages such as voice, tone, phrasing, facial expression, and body language. Listen attentively at the level of feeling and meaning (the intent) to hear the core/essence of what is being conveyed.*

(Whitmore, 2017, p 93)

## Body language/non-verbal communication

When we communicate with another person, it is not only what we say and how we say it we should be aware of but the non-verbal aspects of our communication. This has to do with our stance or bodily posture, proxemics or how close to or far from the other person we place ourselves, our gestures, facial expressions, eye contact, haptics or whether and how we touch the other person. And in making an assessment of what the other person is saying to us, we will probably trust the non-verbal signs rather than the verbal information, albeit at a subconscious level. So someone being honest with us is likely to maintain steady eye contact with us, but shifty eyes or avoidance of eye contact may mean they are being less than honest – this is known as non-verbal leakage. This awareness is important for the practising mentor or coach, who needs to be aware of everything they are communicating to their mentee/coachee as well everything their mentee/coachee is communicating to them. It is no use enthusiastically urging the mentee to continue if the mentor has arms tightly folded, is turned away from the mentee and avoids eye contact – common signals of disengagement.

## Body posture

The way we sit or stand conveys our feelings or attitudes.

### *Activity 11*

- Describe how someone might sit if they were:
  - paying attention;
  - bored;
  - nervous;
  - tired;
  - eager to leave.
- Describe how someone might stand if they were:
  - hostile;
  - ashamed;
  - puzzled;
  - offended;
  - suspicious.

You should have found the above relatively easy to do, which indicates how body posture is capable of quite subtle communication. It follows that when in a mentoring or coaching role, you should be very conscious of body language that suggests openness, enthusiasm and positivity.

## Proxemics

How close you stand or sit to someone depends on the relationship between you: as a rule the closer the relationship, the closer you stand or sit but this is not always true. Consider three situations in which you would not be alarmed if a complete stranger stood or sat very close to you (eg, standing in a lift) and three situations in which you would be alarmed. Furthermore, proxemics is culturally variable: what is acceptable in some cultures may not be in others. There are work situations in which it would be acceptable for complete strangers to be very close to each other and to touch: consider the hairdresser working with a client, a doctor examining a patient, an osteopath at work.

## Gestures

We often use gestures to underline or emphasise what we are saying. Equally, gestures can add to or give feedback.

## *Activity 12*

- How would you interpret the following gestures:
  - someone holding their hands up, palm towards you as you're speaking to them;
  - the head being shaken from side to side while someone else is speaking;
  - the occasional nod by a listener;
  - someone scratching their head while you are talking to them?

### Facial expressions

There are 43 muscles in the human face and between them they are capable of transmitting thousands of subtly different messages. Different parts of the face can change in combination with others.

## *Activity 13*

- Think what happens to the eyebrows alone as the face expresses the following in sequence:
  - anger;
  - puzzlement;
  - no comment;
  - surprise;
  - amazement.

(They should have begun low and gradually been raised!)

- What happens to the mouth when you:
  - realise you have made a mistake;
  - are concentrating;
  - are in pain;
  - are shocked or surprised?

### Eye contact

Whether you look at someone and how you look at them in conversations are very important.

## *Activity 14*

- How would you interpret the following:
  - someone looks downwards continuously as you speak;
  - the listener looks upwards continuously as you speak;
  - someone looks away every time you look at them during a conversation;
  - the listener looks at other things in the room as you are talking to them?

The fact that each of these could have more than one interpretation implies that we should be clear and bold in our body language with our apprentices.

### Haptics

Haptics, communication through touch, is a controversial and complex area. Some families are enormously tactile while others rarely touch one another. Different sorts of touching are acceptable in some cultures and not others. Historically in the UK, the shaking of hands between those of the same and different genders has been acceptable but this becomes more complicated in a multicultural society. Indeed, cultures can be considered as high-contact or low-contact cultures. One of the difficult areas is the potential ambiguity of touching gestures and the interpretation of the significance or intention of touching by the person touched.

As coaches and mentors you should be considering when touch would be appropriate. In such roles, this might be to:

- show support, serving to nurture, reassure, or promise protection;
- show appreciation, to express gratitude for something another person has done;
- indicate inclusion, to draw attention to the act of being together and suggest psychological closeness;
- show affection, to express generalised positive regard beyond mere acknowledgment of the other.

## 4.6 OBSERVATION

Key aspects of the observation of an apprentice in the workplace will be the purpose of the observation, the role the observer takes with regard to the observation and the relationship between observer and observed. Usually, the purpose of the observation will be to assess or evaluate the quality of the observee's work and the Institute for Apprenticeships offers this guidance on the use of observation as an assessment method:

### *What is it?*

*An observation involves an assessor observing an apprentice undertaking a task or series of tasks in the workplace as part of their normal duties ('on-the-job'). This can be complemented by questioning from the assessor during or after the observation. Well-designed observation provides the best and most valid assessment of occupational competence in many occupations.*

### *What is this suitable for?*

*This assessment method is suitable for:*

- *testing knowledge, skills and behaviour holistically*

### *Advantages of this assessment method include:*

- *it is the assessment method most clearly aligned to the working environment and should give the most assurance to employers about an apprentice's competence*

### *What is this not suitable for?*

*This assessment method may be less suitable for:*

- *testing occupations where the skills are less directly observable, for example accountancy, insurance*
- *testing occupations where work takes place over a longer cycle than can reasonably be observed*
- *testing occupations that work in dangerous or restricted work places*

### *Other factors to consider include:*

- *some workplaces may not be suitable for observation to be undertaken in them, or may require additional controls to be put in place for example around security or confidentiality*
- *restricting the desired coverage of an observation could aid comparability but makes 'teaching to the test' a significant risk*
- *observations cannot easily assess aspects of an occupation that are difficult to observe, are rare occurrences*

### *What detail should you include?*

*In order that all end-point assessment organisations (EPAOs) can develop comparable assessment tools, your end-point assessment plan will need to include:*

- *the length of time apprentices will have to undertake the activities*
- *the number and nature of activities that will be need to observed and any that must be observed (if any)*

- *how assessments are to be conducted if something does not happen on the day (through no fault of the apprentice)*
- *the ratio of apprentices to assessors*
- *whether assessors ask the apprentice questions about the activities, and whether this should take place before, during or after the observation*
- *where the observation may or may not take place*
- *how the observation will be made accessible to apprentices with different access requirements*

(Institute for Apprenticeships, 2018)

As a mentor/coach, it is likely that much of your assessment of the apprentice through observation will be of an informal type, probably taking place as part of the normal working day and for formative purposes, as an aid to the apprentice's learning, but there may be occasions when you take a more formal role in order to prepare the apprentice for more summative assessment experiences.

The role taken by the observer will depend upon the context of the observation and the relationship between observer and observed. An external assessor or a supervisor from the workplace organisation is likely to take a detached, non-participatory approach, whereas a mentor/coach will probably take a participatory approach, observing on the job while at the same time giving instructions or asking questions.

It is important for the observer to be aware of the possible effects on the observee of being observed. Particularly relevant here is the Hawthorne Effect or observation effect. The phrase came from H A Landsberger (1968) when he was analysing earlier experiments from 1924 to 1932 at the Hawthorne Works (a Western Electric factory outside Chicago). The Hawthorne Works had commissioned a study to see if its workers would become more productive in higher or lower levels of light. The workers' productivity seemed to improve when changes were made, and deteriorate when the study ended. It was suggested that the productivity gain occurred as a result of the motivational effect on the workers of the interest being shown in them by observers rather than the changes in lighting.

### *Activity 15*

- Consider the ways in which you observe your apprentice. Discuss with them how your observation of them affects their carrying out of work tasks.

## Observation skills

Whether or not you regard yourself as an observant person, you should be able to improve your powers of and skills in observation through the practise of individual skills and through a range of observational activities.

Seeing and hearing are the two senses you probably use most in observing those carrying out work tasks. And as we saw when we considered active listening above, these senses do not operate as passive receptors like cameras and sound recorders. In both cases, we *construct* what we hear and see in a process that involves interpretation. That construction will be affected by a number of factors.

- Our particular view of what good practice is in what we are observing. The authors once observed, in close succession, two (excellent) construction teachers: the first was teaching tiling to apprentices and the second brickwork. When questioned about what the essence of good practice in each activity was, the first teacher thought that good tiling was all about an understanding of 'area', while the second thought good brickwork was underpinned by an appreciation of 'angles'. The authors became aware of how often excellent teaching of vocational practice relied on teachers' awareness of the role of basic skills or maths and English in that practice.
- Our values, ethics and prejudices will often act as the prisms through which we experience the world.
- Our fears and the threats to us can affect our interpretation of what we hear or see.
- The particular interest we have or focus in any one experience.

## *Activity 16*

- Select a room in your house (one which you are not currently in). Describe it in as much detail as you can, detailing items of furniture, other domestic items, wall colour, upholstery. Now go and check. You might not have been that successful! When we live with something every day, it can become invisible (like wallpaper). Now repeat this with another room, only, this time, go to the room and make a conscious effort to remember the items. Go to another room and practise your recall. A better result? We may need to make a conscious effort to observe and recall, particularly in every day contexts such as the home and workplace.
- Think about your most recent journey from home to work or from work to home. Now treat it as a crime scene and answer the following questions.
  - How long did your journey take? At what time did it start? At what time did it finish?
  - How many people did you see on your journey? Describe as many as possible.
  - Did you speak to anyone? Describe them.
  - Did anyone act strangely? If so, how?

- If travelling by car, what were the main colours of other cars on your journey?
- If travelling by public transport, describe who was sitting behind you and next to you?

It is likely that your answers to the questions above were not very precise. What we observe and what we recall depend on the purpose of our observation. If we'd known we were to be a witness before our journey, both observation and recall would have been more accurate.

- You are teaching someone to drive but you haven't got a car yet! Write down instructions about how to drive safely and well.

This should have been very hard work and you probably gave up. When complex processes like driving safely and well become automatic after years of experience, it's very difficult to deconstruct them and describe them as sequences of events.

- Consider some views you have about different aspects of the work tasks you and your apprentice engage in. You might, for example, believe that: 'Most accidents at work (X) are caused by poor health and safety practice (Y).' Generate some X and Y statements about your practice.

In our understanding of work tasks, we have developed, over the years through our training and experience, a whole series of causal relationships, and when we observe others, we may jump to conclusions about what's going on and what might be going wrong in our interpretation of what we are observing based on these causal relationships. We must be aware of these assumptions when interpreting the actions of others.

## 4.7 TEACHING, TUTORING, INSTRUCTION

Your role as a mentor/coach means that much of your interaction with your apprentice is likely to be on a one-to-one basis. This will limit the teaching, tutoring and instruction methods you would be able to use should you need to. Teaching is usually associated with group activity, with the teacher planning the sessions and setting the agenda. Tutoring is more often associated with individuals or small groups, with a broader aim to meet needs in the cognitive, affective and psycho-motor domains and a focus on the student setting the agenda. You will be more concerned with facilitating your apprentice's learning than teaching them for much of the time.

### Professional standards

The Education and Training Foundation (ETF) published the professional standards for teachers and trainers in the education and training sector in 2014. They were intended for all those teaching or training in the sector including learning facilitators such as mentors, assessors and coaches.

## Activity 17

The standards were organised under three headings:

- Professional values and attributes.
- Professional knowledge and understanding.
- Professional skills.

Clearly, some standards will be more relevant for some roles than others. In relation to your role, indicate how far each is relevant, where 1 is high.

*Table 4e Relevance of the Professional Standards*

| Standard | Relevance | | | | |
|---|---|---|---|---|---|
| | 1 | 2 | 3 | 4 | 5 |
| **Professional values and attributes** | | | | | |
| 1. Reflect on what works best in your teaching and learning to meet the diverse needs of learners | | | | | |
| 2. Evaluate and challenge your practice, values and beliefs | | | | | |
| 3. Inspire, motivate and raise aspirations of learners through your enthusiasm and knowledge | | | | | |
| 4. Be creative and innovative in selecting and adapting strategies to help learners to learn | | | | | |
| 5. Value and promote social and cultural diversity, equality of opportunity and inclusion | | | | | |
| 6. Build positive and collaborative relationships with colleagues and learners | | | | | |
| **Professional knowledge and understanding** | | | | | |
| 7. Maintain and update knowledge of your subject and/or vocational area | | | | | |
| 8. Maintain and update your knowledge of educational research to develop evidence-based practice | | | | | |
| 9. Apply theoretical understanding of effective practice in teaching, learning and assessment drawing on research and other evidence | | | | | |
| 10. Evaluate your practice with others and assess its impact on learning | | | | | |
| 11. Manage and promote positive learner behaviour | | | | | |
| 12. Understand the teaching and professional role and your responsibilities | | | | | |

| Professional skills | |
|---|---|
| 13. Motivate and inspire learners to promote achievement and develop their skills to enable progression | |
| 14. Plan and deliver effective learning programmes for diverse groups or individuals in a safe and inclusive environment | |
| 15. Promote the benefits of technology and support learners in its use | |
| 16. Address the mathematics and English needs of learners and work creatively to overcome individual barriers to learning | |
| 17. Enable learners to share responsibility for their own learning and assessment, setting goals that stretch and challenge | |
| 18. Apply appropriate and fair methods of assessment and provide constructive and timely feedback to support progression and achievement | |
| 19. Maintain and update your teaching and training expertise and vocational skills through collaboration with employers | |
| 20. Contribute to organisational development and quality improvement through collaboration with others | |

## Selection of teaching/training methods

The methods we select will depend on a number of factors. First, the nature of our learning objectives will make some methods more suitable than others. Those in the cognitive domain may lend themselves to information given either directly through talk or indirectly through written information. Learning objectives in the affective domain relating, say, to professional behaviour, may be more suitably achieved through discussion or dialogue. And for objectives in the psycho-motor domain relating to cake decoration or upholstery techniques, for example, we may want to use expert demonstration and individual practice.

The motivation and ability of your apprentice will affect your choice of methods. A trainee who needs to be motivated may benefit from approaches that require them to be more active and participative. Any one-to-one method is going to require a high level of participation because they have nowhere to hide! So, a conversation, role play or game will all necessitate full participation. As for ability, it is important that you identify the range of the apprentice's strengths regarding Gardner's 'intelligences', whether it be in logical/mathematical, linguistic, spatial, musical, bodily kinaesthetic or personal intelligences. These may mean that your apprentice has particular learning style preferences as discussed below.

When we looked at learning styles in Chapter 2 we saw that those preferring a visual style respond well to visual stimuli, whether they be PowerPoint demonstrations or video clips.

Auditory learners respond well to auditory stimuli – to podcasts, songs and music. Those preferring a kinaesthetic style are sensitive to touch and movement while verbal learning requires sensitivity to the medium of language, whether it be in written or spoken form. Logical/mathematical learning is rational thinking that seeks to understand the underpinning principles of arguments and systems. Material is absorbed most effectively when it is logically ordered and presented. Learners will want to sort disorganised material into their own logical categories. Intrapersonal learning is most effective when learners are alone rather than with others in social groups. They often say they need to go off and work something out for themselves while interpersonal learning happens best in social groups.

## Teachers' knowledge and subject pedagogy

As Armitage et al show:

> *The types of subject or specialist knowledge a teacher in the lifelong learning sector might require could include:*
>
> - *factual, empirical information;*
> - *an understanding of key principles;*
> - *personal beliefs or a stance on what the subject comprises, how it should be taught or learned;*
> - *an awareness of current practice in the specialism;*
> - *the ways in which a specialism relates to wider social, environmental concerns;*
> - *knowledge of key current developments in the specialism;*
> - *knowledge of the literacy, numeracy and ICT requirements of the specialism;*
> - *an awareness of new and emerging technologies;*
> - *an understanding of key transferable skills*
> - *knowledge of where available resources may be obtained.*
>
> (Armitage et al, 2011, p 96)

The resources that you can access in the section that follows were produced as part of a project based at the School of Education and Professional Development at the University of Huddersfield (Gatsby Foundation, 2018). The materials are aimed at vocational teachers in FE but will be equally applicable in your work situation. It might also be helpful for you to see the approaches that may be taking place as part of your apprentice's off-the-job training.

> ***Pedagogy as decision-making***
>
> *[The team's] broad definition of pedagogy is that it describes how teachers explain the decisions they make in relation to a particular curriculum or body of knowledge (in this case occupational science, engineering and technology) and in relation to a particular student or group of students. It is not 'just what teachers do'.*
>
> (Gatsby Foundation, 2018)

## *Activity 18*

Follow the link www.gatsby.org.uk/education/programmes/teacher-education-in-FE, then the further link below 'Materials from the programme are now available'. Now click the square 'ITE Trainee' below 'Start your journey'. Click the boxes 'Pedagogy as decision-making 1–5' and consider the related Reflections.

### *Pedagogical Content Knowledge (PCK)*

*The concept of Pedagogical Content Knowledge (PCK) was developed by Lee Shulman [Shulman, 1986, 1987; Shulman and Shulman, 2004] in the mid-1980s. He argued that, on top of subject knowledge and general pedagogical skills, teachers must know how to teach topics in ways that learners can understand. So they need to know what makes learning specific topics easy or difficult. This includes appreciating what preconceptions students might have and knowing the best strategies to address any misconceptions.*

(Gatsby Foundation, 2018)

## *Activity 19*

- Click the boxes 'Pedagogical Content Knowledge 6–11' and consider the related Reflections.

### *Content representation*

*A [content representation or] CoRe is constructed by asking teachers to identify the 'big ideas' associated with teaching a topic to a particular group of students. These big ideas become the horizontal axis of a CoRe and are analysed in different ways through prompts listed on the vertical axis. The prompts relate to two areas of a teacher's decision making: curriculum decisions and instructional decisions. The first area contains questions such as 'What do you intend the students to learn?' and 'Why is it important for the students to know this?' The second includes 'Knowledge about students' thinking' and 'Teaching approaches'.*

(Gatsby Foundation, 2018)

## *Activity 20*

- Click the boxes 'Content Representation 9–11' and consider the related Reflections.

***Occupational identity***

*Subject-specialist pedagogy helps develop occupational identity. It does so explicitly by teaching the behaviour and codes of conduct expected in particular professional settings. It also does so implicitly, by using the types of learning processes that are strongly characteristic of the specialism. For example, workshops or labs are used not only to develop knowledge and skills but also to instil attitudes and orientations suitable to occupational roles in science, engineering and technology.*

(Gatsby Foundation, 2018)

## Activity 21

- Click the boxes 'Occupational Identity 12–15' and consider the related Reflections.

***Re-contextualisation***

*The context of an education or training programme is different from the context of the workplace (for example, a laboratory) – while a workshop is related to the real-life context, they are not the same. For effective vocational learning, the teacher must help the learner to move between these contexts.*

*This process is called re-contextualisation, and the teacher is re-contextualising by:*

- *Selecting course content*
- *Selecting teaching, learning and assessment strategies*
- *Relating learning to occupational requirements*
- *Organising work experience and relating work-based and college-based learning*
- *Maintaining a direct 'line of sight to work' whilst meeting the needs of learners.*

*The learner is re-contextualising by:*

- *Recognising elements of course content in workplace practices*
- *Applying what they learn in college to what they do in the workplace*
- *Bringing workplace practice back to the college.*

(Gatsby Foundation, 2018)

## Activity 22

- Click box 16 and consider the related Reflections.

## 4.8 YOUR ACTION PLAN 4

### *Activity 23*

- Complete the action plan below based on the activities in this chapter. Table 4f is available electronically at www.criticalpublishing.com/the-new-apprenticeships.

*Table 4f Your action plan 4*

| **Issue** | **Proposed actions** | **Responsibility for actions** | **Intended targets/ outcomes** | **Timing** |
|---|---|---|---|---|
| 4.1 Models of mentoring and coaching | Eg, coaching skills I need to practise | Myself | Rounded skills as a coach | One year |
| 4.2 Emotional intelligence | Eg, emotional competencies I need to develop | Myself | Competencies recognised by others | One year |
| 4.3 Building rapport, trust and respect | Eg, what more could I do to build better rapport, trust and confidence? | Myself | Positive response from apprentice | One year |
| 4.4 Questioning | Eg, questioning skills I need to enhance | Myself | Positive response from apprentice | One year |
| 4.5 Active listening | Eg, are there aspects of my body language I can improve? (I keep looking at my watch while someone is giving answers) | Myself | Feedback from others | One year |
| 4.6 Observation | Eg, what are the contexts in which I need to improve my observation skills? | Myself | Feedback from others | One year |
| 4.7. Teaching, tutoring, instruction | Eg, how can I improve my subject pedagogy? | Myself | Feedback from others | One year |

# 5 Assessment of achievement

**CHAPTER CONTENT**

This chapter covers:



## 5.1 FEATURES AND PRINCIPLES OF ASSESSMENT

### Features of assessment

Assessment can be formal or informal. An examination is perhaps the most formal of assessment strategies, with invigilators keeping a watchful eye over candidates working in silence in a large hall or a driving examiner formally addressing the examinee and making requests to make specific manoeuvres. At the other extreme, a plumber could suggest informally to her mate that it might be better if a wrench were held in a particular way. Formative assessment is intended to support learning – a brickwork tutor advises a student on the application of mortar – while summative assessment is meant to gather information about achievement, as in the end-point assessment of apprentices. Assessment can be subjective or objective. My judgement about whether a painting is good art will depend on a number of things about *me*, whether I favour figurative art, value drawing craftsmanship, rather than the painting itself or the painter. In that respect it is a highly subjective judgement. However, a multiple choice test of factual information will be objective – multiple choice tests are often called 'objective tests'. Assessment can be continuous or terminal, taking place during or at the end of a period of learning. The focus of assessment might be on the process of learning – how an individual worked out the solution to a maths problem, rather than on the product of learning – the answer they eventually came up with. Assessment can be internal – carried out by a student's own teachers or tutors, for example – or external, set by an external examining or awarding body.

### *Activity 1*

- You and your apprentice should attempt to recall two positive experiences of being assessed and two negative experiences. Now discuss what made the positive experiences positive and the negative experiences negative.

One of the aspects of a positive experience of assessment could have been that you were successful and conversely, of a negative experience, that you were unsuccessful. And when you recall such experiences, it is usually the emotion of the memory that makes it so vivid and unforgettable. We should not underestimate the power of the emotional impact on learners of positive or negative experiences of assessment. Thorough preparation and an understanding of exactly what was required of you were probably positive aspects, as was a sense that the assessment was a fair (or unfair) test of your learning (*'No questions on vitamins, which I knew backwards!'*). One Master's graduate recalled, many years ago, at the end of her course, going to collect her 25,000-word dissertation from her professor. He reached for it from a shelf and returned it to her. She looked inside for some sort of written feedback or mark sheet but there was none. 'So,' she asked rather embarrassed and frustrated 'what did you think of it?' 'Thin,' he replied. Minimal or negative feedback can be thoroughly demoralising.

## Principles of assessment

### Referencing

The referencing of assessment denotes the type of yardstick or measure being applied through the assessment. Individuals in a group are each asked to stand and sing the verse of a song. At the end of the process, the assessor points to individuals: 'You sang the verse better than anybody in the group and you [pointing to someone else] were the worst, I'm afraid. You were second best, you were third... [and so on].' The assessor here was using norm referencing because they were measuring each performance and ranking them against others taking into consideration the norm for this particular group. When you had '10th out of 29' on your school report, your teacher was using norm referencing.

With another group, the assessor points to each individual after their performance and gives them a mark: 7/10, 56 per cent or B+. They are using grade referencing or placing them on a scale of numbers or letters.

With a different group, the assessor gives the following feedback after each sung verse. They might say: 'I thought your enunciation was very crisp and there was a lot of feeling expressed. You sang in tune and made good contact with your audience.' The assessor here is using criterion referencing because they are measuring the performance by applying a set of criteria to it, not comparing it to other performances.

Grade referencing and criterion referencing can be and are often combined:

| | |
|---|---|
| Enunciation 7/10 | Pitch 8/10 |
| Emotion 7/10 | Audience Communication 8/10 |

Total 30/40 or 75 per cent

All end-point assessment of apprentices' achievement is expected to be grade referenced.

> ***Grading***
>
> *3.17 All apprenticeship standards should be graded, with at least one level above a pass to recognise exceptional performance in each assessment method and across the standard as a whole. For example, pass and distinction or pass, merit and distinction. A pass must represent full occupational competence in the occupation, with higher grades representing achievement over and above the standard.*
>
> *3.18 You must include clear grading descriptors in your assessment plan. These set out what is required of an apprentice to achieve each grade you specify. Even where we have granted a grading exemption, a clear descriptor must set out what apprentices must demonstrate in order to achieve a pass. When setting out the grading criteria check that they are sufficiently detailed to ensure consistent interpretation. Avoid using words such as 'good', 'excellent' or 'in-depth' without examples of what this means.*
>
> *3.19 The grades from each assessment method must be aggregated to obtain an apprentice's overall grade. The overall grade needs to take into account the way different assessment methods have been graded and whether the apprentice needs to pass each method in order to pass the EPA overall.*
>
> (Institute for Apprenticeships, 2017a, p 26)

Some referencing uses the extent to which someone can achieve something unsupported as a measure, on a scale of dependence – With no help/With some help/With much help, for example. When an athlete compares their performance with their career best, they are using ipsative referencing (Latin *ipse* means 'self') because they are measuring their own performances against one another.

## Validity

If I were to test your driving ability by asking you to discuss a recent journey you have made, then, as an assessment of your driving ability, this would be invalid as it does not measure what it purports to. Far more valid would be for me to accompany you while you drove. Even more valid would be for me to take several trips with you, in different weather conditions, during the day and night, on different sorts of roads, urban and rural. Some argue that the theory part of the current driving test is invalid because driving ability comprises a set of practical skills only. Validity is also related to the extent to which an assessment measures all the aspects of a piece of learning. Some would argue that an exam in which the questions did not cover the whole curriculum was invalid. Validity is also related to the extent to which an assessment has predictive accuracy: will this test give an accurate indication of whether the candidate will actually make a good mechanic in the future?

## Reliability

Reliability is related to the consistency and repeatability of the assessment. If taken by the same person more than once, is a test likely to produce a similar result (assuming that the person concerned has not engaged in any further learning)? Will the same exam, taken by students in different parts of the country but with a similar ability profile, yield the same results? Will all assessors make the same judgement about an individual performance? Individual assessment strategies can be made more reliable in a number of ways. The more clearly the criteria by which the performance is to be judged are spelt out, the more likely it is that assessors will have an agreed understanding of how a performance can meet these criteria. Precise marking schemes can help ensure that a degree of objectivity can be maintained by a range of assessors. And rigorous, frequent and transparent moderation and verification can increase reliability.

## Authenticity and practicability

The authenticity of an assessment relates to the extent that it is carried out in the circumstances under which it would be performed in real life. Being assessed practising serving drinks in a restaurant is more authentic than being assessed serving drinks to peers in a classroom setting. The availability of materials and equipment or of teachers to assess large numbers of students are factors that may affect how practicable a particular assessment strategy is.

## *Activity 2*

**Assessment test**

On the basis of what you've read in this chapter so far, give yourself ten minutes to complete the test below. The test is available electronically at www.criticalpublishing.com/the-new-apprenticeships.

### Complete the gaps

1. A ………… assessment is one that actually measures what it claims to.
2. Assessing driving skills using a two-week open-book exam would be a/an ………… method.

3. The more a technique allows for personal interpretation by the assessor, the less ............ it becomes.
4. Assessment that occurs at intervals throughout the course is described as ............
5. Whereas exams are ............ assessment strategies, open discussion is more ............
6. ............ referencing compares the same student's previous performances with their present one.
7. Assessment concerned with players' accuracy with the ball and passing skills rather than on whether the team won would be focusing on ............
8. Relating an individual student's achievement to that of the group they are a member of is known as ............ referencing.
9. Giving a student a percentage mark would be to use ............ referencing.
10. Dismantling and reassembling an engine in a college motor vehicle workshop is more ............ than looking at a diagram in a classroom but not as ............ as dismantling and re-assembling a car engine in a garage.

The answers are provided at the back of the book.

- What was your mark out of 10?
- Were you pleased, disappointed, surprised by this score?
- Did you have a response when you saw the phrase 'assessment test'?
- Did you think this was a valid and reliable assessment of your understanding of the features and principles of assessment?

This test was given to a group of students following a taught session on the features and principles of assessment. Their marks ranged from 3/10 to 8/10. It is reasonable to assume they were of the same ability level so why the fluctuation in marks? One low scoring student said that because it was a 'test' they had not looked at their notes. No reference was made in the instructions about consulting notes. One of the important aspects of assessment is that we all carry round with us a history of assessment of ourselves that can influence our performance: the low-scoring trainee had a knee-jerk reaction to the word 'test' – this meant an unseen assessment in exam conditions that meant no notes and no books. The word 'test' often has an emotional effect on all of us – the word itself throwing out a challenge. It also reinforces the point made above that being assessed is a highly emotional experience that evokes memories, threats, fears and disappointments.

Was the test a valid and reliable assessment of your understanding of the features and principles of assessment? It could be argued that it was a valid test in that it tested understanding: you could not have filled in the gaps without understanding the key terms and applying them in contexts other than those in which you learned them. On the other hand, it could be argued that it was invalid in that it tested surface rather than deep learning. A more valid test of your deeper learning and understanding would have been for you to have constructed and administered your own assessment according to the features and principles you had learned.

On the face of it, this is a highly reliable test. Each question has clear answers that are either right or wrong and not susceptible to interpretation by assessors and therefore extremely objective. However, we saw above that a lack of clarity of what was required from the student could undermine the objectivity of the most apparently reliable assessment.

## 5.2 ASSESSMENT METHODS

### Selecting assessment methods

In selecting assessment methods, assessors will pay heed to the aims and objectives of the learning being tested, which will strengthen the validity of the assessment. In the case of the assessment of apprenticeships, assessors will consider the knowledge, skills and behaviours set out in the standards for that individual apprenticeship. The assessment methods to be used for end-point assessment are prescribed in what will be a detailed assessment plan to assess whether the candidate has met the standards of the apprenticeship. At the time of writing, the key assessment methods to be used in apprenticeships are, in descending order of current use: portfolio/logbook, professional dialogue, written or online knowledge test, observed practical assessment, interview or panel discussion, project, presentation or showcase, verbal knowledge test (DfE et al, 2017).

*Table 5a Activity 3*

| **Knowledge, skills or behaviours** | **Assessment strategy** |
|---|---|
| 1. Team working skills including listening, negotiation and planning | a. Presentation |
| 2. Knowledge of current legislation and regulation requirements and updates | b. Simulated crisis incident |
| 3. Ability to reflect on own practice | c. Showcase |
| 4. Understanding of the ethical code of practice of own profession | d. Knowledge test |
| 5. Factual recall | e. Professional dialogue |
| 6. Production of well-made craft products | f. Project |
| 7. The capacity to research and apply findings to own practice | g. Interview |
| 8. The ability to discuss aspects of own practice | h. Observed practical assessment |
| 9. The capacity to think quickly on one's feet | i. Portfolio/logbook |
| 10. Skills in communicating with an audience | j. Objective test |

### *Activity 3*

- In Table 5a, match the knowledge, skills or behaviours with what you think is the most appropriate assessment strategy.

  Answers are at the back of the book.

## Portfolio/logbook

To consider a portfolio/logbook as an assessment method in itself is misleading. Since it can be used for such a variety of purposes and vary so much in content, as indicated below, it is more accurate to describe the portfolio as a vehicle for or record of learning that can be assessed using a range of methods. Increasingly, e-portfolios are being used, not just as part of initial training or as part of apprenticeship training but also in continuing professional development activities. They currently appear to be most often used across the education and health sectors. One of the key strengths of the e-portfolio is that it can be accessed from anywhere by a number of parties, as long, of course, as they have permission. So the employer, the off-the-job trainer, the work-based coach or mentor might all have access, communicating with the apprentice and possibly one another. This can ensure that the training is integrated and is therefore more effective, rather than exist as a range of disparate strands. There is a very real tension in the use of portfolios between their function as learning tools and the assessment of their content. Some trainees may see them as less important as other elements of their programme if they are not assessed: conversely, the fact that they are to be assessed may inhibit trainees or make them engage with them in a mechanistic, routine way.

Portfolios usually have the following features.

**1. A personal profile**

This can have a range of content: educational history, previous qualifications, experience, personal attributes and achievements. It might also contain the results of any diagnostic initial assessment, which can give the reader an idea of the individual's starting point in a programme or apprenticeship, facilitating the measurement of progress achieved along the way.

**2. A record of achievement**

This might record the achievement of the individual against the apprenticeship standards or as part of off-the-job training or individual elements of it, such as module outcomes.

**3. A record of the observation of practice**

The principles of observed practical assessment will be considered below but this record is where the outcomes of such assessment by employers, trainers, mentor/coaches can be captured.

**4. A record of the apprentice's observation of other practitioners**

Observing other practitioners' work is a key learning opportunity for apprentices and this record can indicate the extent of their experience and what they have learnt from it.

**5. Records of meetings with mentor/coaches, trainers**

These records may simply note the key points discussed in the meeting. However, these meetings provide ideal opportunities for action planning, noting particularly distance travelled since the last meeting, achievement against targets identified, areas for development and targets identified going forward.

**6. A log of practice**

This can be presented simply as a record of tasks completed, length of time spent on the task and whether checked or signed off. The professional registration for some occupations requires that the length of time in practice is presented (for the achievement of an initial diploma in FE teaching, for example, you would be required to present evidence of 100 hours of teaching, with eight observations of this teaching by a mentor or tutor). However, it could be used as a reflective log and be part of the mentoring cycle described in Section 3.3. So the log might capture the apprentice's reflection on action, answering the questions:

- What does the apprentice notice?
- What are they understanding and how would they develop it?
- What follow-up is needed?

However, the assessment of such reflection is problematic and for it to have validity and reliability there would need to be a detailed rubric or mark scheme, specifying any assessment criteria clearly so that the apprentice knows exactly what is wanted and the assessor what to look for.

**7. A blog or diary**

This differs from the log of practice in that it is a much freer-flowing account of the user's experience and opinions. But it would give a flavour of the user's working practice on a regular day-to-day basis.

**8. Compendium of assignments**

It is usual for the portfolio to contain these or a link to these. Not only does it allow all supervising staff to see what tasks the trainee is completing as part of their programme but if the assignments have been submitted via an electronic submission and assessment system, they are able to see how well the trainee has achieved, how they need to develop and how they have developed.

**9. Visual evidence**

Most e-portfolios allow users to upload photographs or videos, which can present instant visual evidence of an artefact, a learnt process or demonstration of skills.

## Professional dialogue

The Future Apprenticeships course 'End-Point Assessment – Prepare to Deliver' (DfE et al, 2017) defines professional dialogue as '*candidate-led assessment that reveals their knowledge and understanding through the direction and depth of their input. As a result, it is more challenging to assess and grade. Well deployed, it is a highly effective assessment method*'. The course distinguishes between the professional dialogue and the interview: the latter consists of questions and answers whereas the former will begin with very open stimulus questions to generate the dialogue with further extension questions to test the candidate's knowledge. Although the assessor initiates the dialogue, the onus will be on the candidate to demonstrate their knowledge by steering the dialogue.

Professional dialogue can be used in tandem with other assessment methods such as an observation or project debrief but also as a free-standing knowledge assessment. As a method itself, it is ideal as a probing tool to explore the depth of a candidate's knowledge. It is a good method to explore innovative ideas and a candidate's creative potential. Its validity depends on correct implementation and gathering of evidence without unintended leading or bias on the part of the assessor. The professional dialogue may be between the assessor and apprentice or between an employer and apprentice with the assessor as observer.

The course lists the advantages and disadvantages of professional dialogue as an assessment method as shown in Table 5b.

*Table 5b Advantages and disadvantages of professional dialogue*

| **Advantages** | **Disadvantages** |
|---|---|
| • *A flexible form of assessment to cover gaps in evidence from project work, practical assessment or written assignments*<br>• *If conducted well, can evidence behaviour development*<br>• *Particularly good at generating evidence for problem-solving*<br>• *A highly flexible, low risk, low-impact, low cost form of assessment*<br>• *An ideal method for independent or external validation of original assessment* | • *Can provide limited evidence when questions are poorly designed or closed (eliciting a yes/no response) or where repetition occurs, scope is less well defined, or questions are non-stimulating*<br>• *Bad assessments are 'chatty' or mechanical lists of questions, rather than an opportunity to discuss the area of interest*<br>• *Can generate a large quantity of evidence that might be difficult to grade or validate. The skill of the assessor is central to the recording of data. The risk is reduced when combined with audio or video assessment tools. If this is the case, it becomes an ideal format for external validation or independent assessment*<br>• *Qualitative evidence can be difficult to grade and compare across a peer group* |

From DfE et al, 2017

## Scenario

Kiran, Ruhul's mentor, has just observed his level 2 English class on 'Using the phone in occupational contexts'. The professional dialogue is intended to complement the observation: this focused on Ruhul's teaching and management of learning, while the professional dialogue is intended to test learning objectives which it would have been impossible to do through an observation alone:

- Reflect on and effectively evaluate own practice.
- Consider alternative approaches to teaching and learning.
- Identify activities that will develop own practice.
- Consider the effectiveness of behaviour management strategies.

**Kiran:** *OK Ruhul, so how do you think it went? What did you think were strong points of the lesson and what might have gone less well?*

**Ruhul:** *I thought the exercise in which pairs of students sat back to back went really well. They got exactly the difficulties that arose because of the absence of non-verbal communication and the confusion which can be caused as a result about the other person's meaning. I also think they found it fun – there was a lot of laughter during the exercise. And, er, in the simulated calls I also thought they got the importance of the different items you need to include when leaving a message and when it is and when it isn't appropriate to leave a message. But, er, next time, I wouldn't have started with the discussion about whether you use the phone or another form of communication in different situations. The situations I gave them were not sufficiently contextualised and they got confused and anxious about it and – well I'm coming to see more and more that you need to begin a lesson with a powerful stimulus that really motivates and galvanises the students...*

**Kiran:** *OK. I have to say, I was surprised that you didn't use the students' own phones during the lesson.*

**Ruhul:** *That was the first thing I thought about when I was planning it. But, when I looked at each of the learning objectives, it was clear to me that they could best be achieved with all the students in the same room, rather than some of them being in other rooms and calling each other. That would also have caused logistical problems and made it difficult for me to switch strategies quickly.*

**Kiran:** *Why did you completely ignore H's acting up?*

**Ruhul:** *As you might have guessed, this wasn't the first time for H. In the past, I've tried to go down the road of accommodating his boredom by creating activities just for him but it hasn't worked. So, this time I thought I'd ignore him!*

**Kiran:** *And did it work?*

**Ruhul:** *[Laughs] No – he just got worse, didn't he?*

**Kiran:** *What would help with your behaviour management?*

**Ruhul:** *Frankly, I'm just experimenting at the moment. When I was on the training programme, I learnt so much from other students and how they dealt with problems. I wonder... maybe observe colleagues and see how they deal with behaviour problems and look around for courses, CPD that I could attend...*

### *Activity 4*

- Write a short report on the extent to which this professional dialogue provides evidence of Ruhul meeting the learning objectives.

## Knowledge test

There is a range of knowledge tests that might be used to assess apprentices' achievements. Some of the key ones are described below.

### Short answer test

Short answer questions are ideal when the learning objectives require a grasp of facts, concepts, principles or applied knowledge. There are two types of short answer questions. There are direct questions that invite candidates to respond in a few sentences or a short paragraph. For example:

1. *Which type of document details the type of fixings to be used for a soil or vent pipe?*
2. *How can stair carpets be protected from damage while carrying out the replacement of a bathroom suite?*
3. *What type of document details the exact price that a plumbers' merchant will supply materials for?*
4. *The distance between two tees in a pipeline measures 850mm. The x dimension of each tee (centre line of tee to position of end of pipe) is 12mm. What is the required length of pipe?*
5. *What is the maximum diameter that a hole can be drilled in a timber floor joist?*

**Answers:**

1. *This type of information would be contained in a job specification.*
2. *By covering them with dust sheets, taking care at all times to avoid tripping hazards.*
3. *A quotation is used for fixed prices.*
4. *X dimension = 12mm, for the two fittings 2 × 12 = 24mm. Length of pipe is 850 – 24 = 826mm.*
5. *Maximum diameter of a hole 0.25 of the depth of the joist.*

(Qs and As from Thompson, 2007)

There are short-answer questions that require gaps to be completed, such as those in Activity 2 above.

## Multiple choice test

Multiple choice tests invite the candidate to select one correct answer from a choice of usually four or five items. There is the stem or question itself and then the correct answer, an answer very close in meaning to the correct answer, the 'distractor', and then two or three other possible answers. Multiple choice tests are ideal for testing factual recall or comprehension/understanding.

1. *The different phases of work that need to take place to complete the construction of a new dwelling are detailed in a:*
   a. *Job specification*
   b. *Work programme*
   c. *Maintenance schedule*
   d. *Site drawing*
2. *A plumbers' merchant should provide which one of the following documents when supplying materials to a private dwelling?*
   a. *Invoice*
   b. *Order*
   c. *Delivery note*
   d. *Quotation*

**Answers:**

1. *b*
2. *c*

(Qs and As from Thompson, 2007)

The question should be unambiguous and there should only be one right answer. The question should be clearly and simply stated so that the candidate can understand it. The distractor should be close to the correct answer and a plausible alternative. The distractors in 1 and 2 above are c and a. What makes them good distractors? The answers should be brief and usually the same length. The position of each correct answer should be varied (not all the first or last, for example). Avoid trick questions ('None of these is correct').

### Matching test

Matching tests are used when concepts or ideas need to be defined, identified, or classified. Table 5a is a matching exercise with knowledge, skills or behaviours matched with appropriate assessment strategies. Only one match should be possible for each item. If more than one is possible then knowledge is not being properly tested. An advantage of a matching test is that it has the quality of a game or puzzle and this can be motivating for the candidate.

## Essays

Essays are usually used to test more complex knowledge and understanding. The criteria you specify to assess the essay will give both the candidate and the assessor clarity about the knowledge, understanding or abilities the essay is testing.

### *Activity 5*

- Match each criterion in Table 5c with an essay title.

  Suggested pairings can be found at the back of the book.

*Table 5c Activity 5*

| **Criterion** | **Essay title** |
|---|---|
| 1. The accurate description of a process | a. 'The key aspects of good health, safety and welfare practice in your occupational role' |
| 2 The construction of a sound argument | b. 'Soundness testing of central heating systems' |
| 3. The ability to persuade | c. 'Advantages/disadvantages of instruction versus discovery learning' |
| 4. Analysing complex ideas | d. 'Reasons we should leave the European Union' |
| 5. The capacity to describe and explain clearly | e. 'This house believes all sports involving animals are cruel' |
| 6. The ability to compare and contrast | f. 'Major triggers of high blood pressure' |
| 7. The identification of cause and effect processes | g. 'My philosophy of education' |

One of the challenges of assessing essays is making judgements about the quality of knowledge and understanding demonstrated. The reliability of such assessment can be increased by the use of a mark scheme, such as the one below.

**'Soundness testing of central heating systems'**

**Mark scheme**

| | |
|---|---|
| Comprehensiveness of account of visual inspection | 5 |
| Correctness of sequence of test for leaks | 5 |
| Correctness of procedure for pressure testing | 5 |
| Fullness of detail of final system checks | 5 |
| TOTAL | 20 |

## Observed practical assessment

### In this book so far

Observation as an assessment strategy has already been dealt with in some detail in previous chapters. In Chapter 3, Section 3.4, mentor Kiran McGregor accompanies healthcare assistant Danielle Downer on a home visit and observes her managing a client. Danielle is then given a feedback summary which is subsequently developed as a record of learner progress.

In Chapter 3, Section 3.6, when PGCE student Aretha Macdonald is observed, you saw how important the pre- and post-observation conversations between Aretha and her coach were in complementing the observation in the coaching process.

In the scenario in Section 4.4, the role of questioning was emphasised in the pre- and post-observation conversation between Dean, the cabin crew apprentice, and his coach.

In Section 4.6, you saw that key aspects of the observation of an apprentice in the workplace were the purpose of observations, the role the observer takes with regard to the observation and the relationship between observer and observed. Usually, the purpose of the observation will be to assess or evaluate the quality of the observee's work. Attention was also paid here to observation skills and it was emphasised that these can be improved through practice.

### *Activity 6*

- Go back to the sections above and note the key points you learned about observation as a practical assessment strategy from them.

## Further issues in observation

### 1. Participation or detached observer?

In the former, the observation is likely to be taking place as you and your observee are completing a job. This may involve you observing *while* you are co-working, co-tasking and/or then stopping once the task has been completed, standing back and contemplating the completed task. Alternatively, you may take the more formal role of a detached observer. An advantage of the participative approach is that it is natural, not contrived for the purpose of the observation and there is likely to be minimal observation effect on the apprentice. An advantage of the detached approach is that it is likely to be more objective and therefore more reliable.

### 2. How to measure?

Kiran McGregor's feedback to Danielle Downer was a straightforward narrative account of saying what she thought she saw as in a witness statement in NVQ assessment. Alternatively, you might wish to use a narrative account but assess/evaluate as you go – say what you saw/say what you think of it. Or you may wish to give a narrative account and leave any judgement of quality or evaluation to the end of this account.

You might want to take a more structured approach to the evaluation in which you make your judgements in predetermined categories – these may be assessment criteria or selected standards for assessing the apprenticeship or parts of the process. In this case, you will need to decide how you are going to record your observations. Clearly, recording your judgements about part of the process is most straightforward because it allows you to assess/evaluate as you go. Table 5d provides a template for how you might do this.

*Table 5d Template for recording judgements*

| **Parts of process** | **Comments** |
|---|---|
| Comprehensiveness of account of visual inspection | |
| Correctness of sequence of test for leaks | |
| Correctness of procedure for pressure testing | |
| Fullness of detail of final system checks | |
| With assessment criteria or standards, you may need to jump around from one category to another as the observation proceeds. | |
| **Criteria** | **Comments** |
| Understand testing of cold water, hot water central heating systems | |
| Demonstrate correct approach to fault diagnosis and repair techniques | |
| Understand maintenance procedures | |
| Understand servicing procedures | |

## 3. Authenticity

On the whole, the more authentic the observation setting, the more valid and reliable the assessment. This is because real work tasks are being assessed in a real-life setting. Obviously, there are limits to how authentic the assessment can be - there may be health and safety issues that limit authenticity, for example. Assessors need to think hard whether what may appear to be authentic is undermined by the strategy adopted. Take this scenario, for example:

### Scenario

Effie is being cash till trained in a real retail environment. Effie is at the till and the supervisor/trainer stands behind her. Effie has scanned the customer's goods through the till.

**Effie:** *So, that'll be £35 please.*

[The customer proffers her payment card.]

**Supervisor/trainer:** [to Effie] *Hang on - what do we need to do first?* [to the customer] *Sorry...*

**Customer:** [to Effie] *Don't you worry, take your time.*

**Effie:** [to supervisor/trainer] *Oh yeah...* [to customer] *Would you like any cash back?*

**Customer:** [to Effie] *No thanks.*

**Supervisor/trainer:** [to Effie] *And?*

**Effie:** *Oh right...* [to customer] *Have you got a rewards card?*

[The customer shakes her head. Effie correctly rings up the sale and gives the customer her change and her vouchers.]

**Customer:** [to Effie] *Bye! Well done.*

If this was an assessed event above, how authentic was it? The authors witnessed very similar events when assessing vocational students on work placement. The supervisor/assessor felt she had to be that close to Effie so that she could assess what she was doing, vital in a real-life situation, she argued. She also felt she had to make the interventions she did, otherwise the customer would not have been properly served. For her part, the customer cottons on, makes allowances for Effie and tolerates the slower service. All of this undermines the authenticity of what is potentially an authentic, real-life situation.

It could be argued that it would have been better for Effie to have been more thoroughly till trained in a simulated environment so that she was unlikely to make basic mistakes, with the actual real-life assessment being carried out by a secret shopper/assessor or a trainer observing from a distance far enough away not to alert customers.

### 4. Electronic observation

Consideration needs be given to whether an assessment can be electronically observed as well as or instead of human observation. There is a limit to what the camera or a microphone can pick up even if they are carefully technically operated. Remote electronic observation is becoming increasingly popular and there are some very sophisticated packages on the market. Of course, electronic recording can increase the reliability of observed assessment by giving access to what can be a subjective form of assessment to other assessors, internal and external verifiers.

## The interview

The interview consists of a series of questions asked by the interviewer(s) of the respondents from whom certain answers will be expected, rather than the more flexible, free-flowing interaction of the professional dialogue. The interview can be face to face or be held at a distance. The advantage of the former is that interactions between interviewer and interviewee are more straightforward and there is less chance of miscommunication than there might be using, for example, Skype, Face Time or video conferencing. The interview is a good method for testing knowledge and understanding and in this respect could be seen to be the oral equivalent of a short answer test. It can be used to complement or triangulate with other forms of assessment such as the portfolio or an observed practical assessment. Indeed, the interview questions could focus entirely, say, on the portfolio brought in, with candidates not simply answering questions but also illustrating their answers with examples of work already completed. The questions should be clearly formulated, free from ambiguity and use language that the interviewee would be expected to comprehend at their level. Agreeing in advance on the nature and number of questions is fairer to all candidates and is likely to increase the reliability of the interview as an assessment method. It is important that the interview take place in an environment where both interviewer and interviewee are comfortable. The interviewer may use a series of prompts such as photographs as a way of stimulating answers. The interview can be conducted one-to-one or be a panel interview. An advantage of the former is that it is less daunting for the interviewee who can concentrate on producing correct answers rather than be inhibited by the formality of the occasion. On the other hand, a panel interview can enhance the reliability of the method: panel members can concentrate on the answers being given to others' questions; there is the opportunity to discuss a candidate's performance after the interview. A decision will need to be made on whether candidates are given advance notice of the questions.

A decision will also need to be made regarding how/if the interview is to be recorded. Asking questions, listening to the answers and note-taking require a highly complex set of skills. However, the process of note-taking means that the assessor will be making decisions about what is worth writing down and therefore already engaging in the assessment process during the interview. An audio or video record will allow the interviewer to give their full attention to the candidate. And the recording, shared with other assessors, can be an aid to standardisation and moderation. However, a microphone in front of them or a camera trained on them can inhibit even the most confident of candidates. The good interviewer is one who is attentive to the candidate, maintaining eye contact and giving the candidate appropriate prompts, and is sensitive to the candidate's feelings.

## Project, presentation, showcase

These three methods are often closely related in practice. Although projects, presentations and showcases can be free-standing, a presentation or showcase may be that of project findings or artefacts. They can also be related to some of the methods above: in many assessment plans, a presentation is often paired with and followed by a professional dialogue or interview between a panel and the apprentice.

### Project

The Institute of Apprenticeships *Assessment Method Guide* (Institute for Apprenticeships, 2017b) suggests that

> *using a project as an assessment method involves the apprentice completing a significant and defined piece of work after the gateway. This could involve a written essay, or in practical occupations, producing an item (an 'apprentice piece') which an assessor can review and mark.*

It is an ideal method where the work cycle is too long to be reasonably observed and can test knowledge, skills and behaviour holistically. End-point assessors using this method should include in their assessment plan:

- the scope of the project and how this would be agreed between the assessment organisation and employer;
- how long apprentices will have to complete the project and when they would be expected to finish it;
- a word limit (for a written assignment or essay) or any other constraints as appropriate;
- supervision and verification arrangements that need to be in place and how the assessor will gain assurance that the work has been completed by the apprentice;
- the format in which the evidence will be required;
- how the project will be made accessible to apprentices with different access requirements.

The use of projects in existing assessment plans indicates that they are most appropriate where the occupational work involves a process ending with a product, where research and enquiry are fundamental to the process or where the product is an event or series of events or an artefact. Examples include:

***Accountancy/taxation professional level 7***

*Apprentices will prepare a report based on their own recent relevant experience for each of the set requirements. Within the report, each response would have a minimum word limit of 700 words and a maximum word limit of 1,000 words. Apprentices would be asked to structure each of their responses to include:*

- *background and context to the scenario identified in the question;*
- *a description of their role, responsibilities and of the actions within the specific scenario;*
- *an evaluation of the particular professional skills and behaviours used and developed in the context of the scenario(s);*
- *a critical examination of the lessons learned.*

***Level 3 boat builder apprenticeship***

*Location: The assignment should take place in the workshops or other locations where the apprentice typically works, with access to all the appropriate equipment, machinery, relevant tools and consumables for working safely with boat building equipment and marine engineering materials.*

*Time: The project activity should take no longer than 5 days (40hrs) to complete. This can be either in one block of time or spread over a longer period depending on the nature of the activity.*

*Security of work: During the assignment any unfinished task/work in progress must be kept in a secure environment to avoid damage, theft or possible plagiarism.*

*Supervision: Apprentices should be able to work autonomously to complete the task, reflecting usual working practices.*

***Cyber intrusion analyst***

*A project [will give] the apprentice the opportunity to undertake a business-related project over a one-week period away from the day to day workplace.*

***Level 3 event assistant***

*The project must cover:*

- *a commission from a client or organisational brief, so an apprentice can demonstrate how they have responded to the brief;*
- *the use of software packages to create word processing and spreadsheet documents;*
- *contribution to reports, event project plans and written presentations for clients;*

- *the use of a range of event technology platforms and in-house bespoke software systems and databases;*
- *how conclusions are drawn to choose venues that may be suited to a particular event based on clients' needs;*
- *each aspect of event logistics: the venue, delegate management, transportation, accommodation, catering;*
- *liaison with event suppliers to combine and contribute to deliver an event;*
- *how the onsite team at an event collaborated to ensure that the client's and all the delegates needs are met.*

***Fashion and textiles pattern cutter level 3***

*Apprentices must complete a project based on the production of a master pattern(s). The project has three components:*

- *project report and evidence;*
- *fit session observation;*
- *questioning.*

*Independent assessors must assess the evidence from the project report and evidence, fit session observation and questioning synoptically against the KSBs assessed by this method as shown in annex A, using the grading criteria in annex B and assign a grade.*

*Project requirements*

*The master pattern(s) must:*

- *require one set of basic blocks with a minimum of three components;*
- *cover basic patterns of different styles, comprising of 20 pattern pieces in total +/− 10% or one complex pattern comprising of 20 pattern pieces +/− 10%;*
- *require a competent pattern cutter six hours to draft the final master pattern(s) (not including the production of prototype patterns)*

(Institute for Apprenticeships, 2017c)

## Presentation/showcase

A presentation involves an apprentice presenting to an assessor, or panel of assessors, on a particular topic (Institute for Apprenticeships, 2017b). It is suitable for:

- testing understanding of a subject;
- testing knowledge and skills in an occupation that cannot be directly observed easily;
- testing certain skills and behaviours directly – for example the ability to present publicly, interact with others and capacity for self-reflection, if these are required by the occupational standard.

The Strategic Development Network's (2016) guidance on presentations is as follows. The presentation/showcase comprises a short presentation including slides, notes, handouts and input from the apprentice. The technology and format of the presentation may vary. The presentation is used to demonstrate an understanding beyond knowledge and factual recall and can allow this knowledge to be explored, particularly if the assessment includes a question session with the apprentice afterwards. The apprentice is asked to devise a presentation that could be in a variety of formats to describe their work project, findings, learning progress and knowledge learned in a formal, but relaxed setting. This normally includes an introduction, some key input, with an opportunity for exploratory questions at the end. Duration can vary, but normally increases with the complexity of the project and occupational level. The presentation/showcase assesses applied knowledge of a project or topic – it allows the apprentice to demonstrate their understanding within the context of their work and job role.

The presentation/showcase can also be used to assess some behaviours, especially written and verbal communication as well as understanding of a topic or area of study. Recording verbal qualitative data is vital (video, audio or text) as it then allows the assessor to grade the apprentice (pass/fail) and determine whether higher-level grades have been achieved. It also provides a robust evidence base to justify and moderate the assessor's decision.

> *The advantages of this assessment method are that the apprentice-led nature of the assessment gives the apprentice a live opportunity to demonstrate their knowledge and understanding. If set up and conducted well, the assessment will [facilitate the assessment of] knowledge, and aspects of skills and behaviours (in context) all under one assessment component, and will allow effective triangulation with other assessment methods.*
>
> *The risks of this assessment method are [that] not all apprentices respond positively or confidently to this form of assessment and this can lead to a lack of consistency in grading and achievement. The 'high-stakes' nature of end-point assessment can compound this issue. With frameworks, the trainer-assessor had built a relationship with the apprentice over a period of a year or more. Now the assessor is a stranger (independent of the training), with no prior relationship with the apprentice. The assessor will need to be able to put the apprentice at ease from the start, allowing them sufficient space to demonstrate their understanding.*
>
> *Apprentices may also be tempted to dedicate a disproportionate amount of time and resource in the preparation and practice of their presentation/showcase, which can then impinge on their preparation time and performance in other parts of the end-point assessment. They will need to take care not to spend too much of their preparation time on how the presentation is done or looks rather than what is presented (which is what ultimately will demonstrate their competence). In preparation, on-programme trainers will want to have a clear understanding of the grading and assessment brief, so the apprentice can ensure their presentation covers all required areas and allows the apprentice to demonstrate higher-level*

*knowledge. This form of assessment lends itself to independent testing, and in some cases can be conducted remotely or online.*

(Strategic Development Network, 2016)

## 5.3 QUALITY ASSURANCE OF ASSESSMENT

You saw in Chapter 3 that your role as a mentor to the new apprentice is likely to be complex.

*Although most likely to be a fellow employee of the apprentice, it is possible that you may be a member of the training provider organisation or its associates. Indeed, any one apprentice may have more than one mentor in the different organisations supporting their apprenticeship. Furthermore, because of this complexity and the varied patterns of off-the-job and on-the-job training, it is possible that you will, as well as mentor, be acting in other roles with them – such as trainer for your employer.*

It follows that your part in the assessment of the apprentice and in the quality assurance of that assessment will be complex as well and depend on the assessment requirements of that specific apprenticeship as well as the overall quality assurance arrangements for it. Each apprenticeship has an end-point assessor organisation (EPAO) independent of the employer, the training provider(s) organisation and its associates. Each apprenticeship also has an external quality assurance provider independent of the employer, the training provider(s) organisation and its associates *and* the EPAO.

According to the Institute for Apprentices:

*external quality assurance should explore the following areas for each standard.*

1. *Standards and assessment plans*
   a. *standards and assessment plans are and will continue to be fit for purpose*
   b. *the Assessment Plan is valid and cost-effective in practice*
   c. *there is use of a suitable range of assessment methods*
   d. *assessment instruments and assessments are valid across a range of real work settings and for employers of any size and in any sector;*
   e. *assessment methods are clearly aligned to the application of specific skills, knowledge and behaviours*
   f. *assessment is carried out as far as is practicable synoptically and that this applies to at least one method of assessment of skills and knowledge*
   g. *assessment is carried out independently in practice. This means that both the organisation and the individual assessors are independent of the delivery of training and employment of the apprentice;*
   h. *individual assessment instruments/methods are fit for purpose.*

2. *End-point assessment*

   a. *assessments are operating effectively and achieving the desired outcomes*

   b. *grading is applied accurately and consistently*

   c. *access to assessment is fair*

   d. *assessors are fully occupationally competent as set out in the assessment plan*

   e. *assessors' knowledge is up-to-date as set out in the assessment plan*

   f. *sufficient assessors are available*

   g. *all requirements of the standard in terms of achievement of gateways and mandatory qualifications and requirements are achieved prior to sign off and the employer makes the final decision on the readiness of the apprentice for EPA*

   h. *assessment is reliable and comparable across different EPAOs, employers, places, times and assessors*

3. *End-point assessment organisations*

   a. *internal quality assurance processes carried out by the EPAOs meet the requirements set out in the assessment plan*

   b. *employers are choosing EPAOs and have enough information to make an informed choice*

   c. *each EPAO has arrangements to collect and action feedback from apprentices and employers*

   d. *accurate records are kept and data is held securely with appropriate protocols in place*

   e. *information provided and fees charged are clear and transparent*

   f. *retakes, resits, appeals and complaints handling are operated effectively; and*

   g. *delivery of EPA by the EPAOs is efficient and effective including:*

      - *timeliness of assessment windows*
      - *booking and management of assessment*
      - *marking/remote assessment*
      - *resources for assessment*
      - *evidence gathering and record keeping*
      - *issue of results and feedback*
      - *confidentiality*
      - *certification including its timeliness and checking any requirements.*

(Institute for Apprenticeships, 2017d)

It is possible that in the preparation of your apprentice for end-point assessment through on-programme formative assessment, you may be affected by the quality assurance processes described above, but it is more likely that you will be involved in the internal quality assurance of this formative assessment. You may or may not already have been involved in these processes, most likely as part of a vocational qualification your current mentee (if you have one) is following. However, the key QA activities involved are likely to be as follows.

## Moderation or standardisation

This is the process that ensures that marking or grading criteria are being applied accurately by different assessors. The process usually involves a meeting of these assessors, each of whom will scrutinise a number of sample pieces of work. The work is selected to provide a range of levels of achievement. These have already been marked/graded but this outcome is not available at this stage to the assessors. The assessors then share their findings and any discrepancies between assessors can be discussed and differences resolved. At HE level, two processes may be involved in moderation. Work is usually first- and second-marked by assessors – the second marking may be 'blind', with the second marker unaware of the judgement of the first marker. Moderation will then take place as the first and second markers reveal and resolve their judgements. Most university awards will have an external examiner, part of whose job it is to ensure that assessment criteria are being applied consistently and fairly.

## Verification

While moderation ensures that marking or grading criteria are being applied accurately by different assessors, internal and external verifiers consider whether the assessment policies and processes as a whole are being fairly and consistently followed in line with awarding organisation practice. They will do so by: considering candidates' work; observing and discussing assessment practice with assessors; interviewing candidates; scrutinising assessor feedback; assessor record-keeping.

### *Activity 7*

- What are the key challenges for moderation and verification with relation to the major methods used for the assessment of apprentices:
  - portfolio/logbook;
  - professional dialogue;
  - knowledge test;
  - observed practical assessment;
  - interview or panel discussion;
  - project;
  - presentation or showcase?

## 5.4 YOUR ACTION PLAN 5

### *Activity 8*

- Complete the action plan below based on the activities in this chapter. Table 5e is available electronically at www.criticalpublishing.com/the-new-apprenticeships.

*Table 5e Your action plan 5*

| **Issue** | **Proposed actions** | **Responsibility for actions** | **Intended targets/ outcomes** | **Timing** |
|---|---|---|---|---|
| 5.1 Features and principles of assessment | Eg, devising an assessment which meets the key principles of assessment | Myself, training partners | Positive response from quality assurers | One year |
| 5.2 Assessment methods | Eg, experience of the key methods of assessment used with apprentices | Myself, training partners, employer trainers | Positive response from quality assurers | One year |
| 5.3 Quality assurance of assessment | Eg, participation in both moderation and verification processes | Myself, training partners, quality assurers | Positive response from quality assurers | One year |

# Answers

## CHAPTER 3

### Activity 6: How SMART? Suggested answers

1. This is a broad target and therefore scores low on S. Although relatively high in M, A and R, it is not at all time-bound. Score of 3 suggested.
2. Relatively low on specificity – there is no indication of the contexts in which lifting takes place. However, quite high on M – an expert could use criteria to make a judgement about safety and on A and R, given the assistant's role. However, the target is not time specific. Again, score of 3 suggested.
3. Although referring to specific yard duties, there is no indication beyond 'effectively' regarding how well these should be carried out and therefore low on M. Again high for A and R, and for T since the target is time-bound. Score of 4 suggested.
4. This is high on S since the number of common faults in a pillar tap will be limited. High on M since skills demonstrated in diagnosing and rectifying will be specific and measurable and common faults in pillar taps will be small in number. High in A and R – these are basic plumbing activities for the L2 apprentice. Highly time specific as well so a rating of 6 suggested.
5. As in the groom example in 3 above, these are specific duties. However, there is no indication of what might be considered success. They are high in A and R but not time related. Score of 4 suggested.
6. Although specialist duties are mentioned, they are not specified and it is therefore difficult to know whether they have been carried out effectively. A and R are limited because you would have to wait for adverse weather conditions to demonstrate these skills. And 'by the end of the apprenticeship' is hardly time-bound. Score of 2 suggested.
7. The 'characteristics of a variety of fabrics' is rather wide ranging and the level of understanding not clear. A and R are relatively high according to the level of the apprenticeship but, again, 'by the end of the apprenticeship' is not highly time specific. Score of 3 suggested.
8. The relative vagueness of 'quality product' and 'safe for the consumer' limit specificity which also makes these aspects difficult to assess. High in A and R relative to the chef's level of training. There is no time-bound feature. Suggest 3.

9. The complexity of these activities makes them low in S and M but also low in A and R because of the timeframe. Suggest 1.
10. Again, as in 9 above, complexity makes these achievements low in S and M, although, given the timeframe and the graduate level, higher in A and R. Score of 2 suggested.

# CHAPTER 5

## Activity 2: Test answers

1. valid
2. invalid
3. objective
4. continuous
5. formal, informal
6. ipsative
7. process
8. norm
9. grade
10. authentic, authentic

## Activity 3: Suggested matching of the knowledge, skills or behaviours with the most appropriate assessment strategy

1. h
2. d
3. i
4. e
5. j
6. c
7. f
8. g
9. b
10. a

## Activity 5: Criterion/essay title – suggested pairings

1. b
2. d
3. e
4. g
5. a
6. c
7. f

# References


Allison, D (2017) How to Fix Degree Apprenticeships. *FE Week*, 5 October. [online] Available at: https://feweek.co.uk/2017/10/05/how-to-fix-degree-apprenticeships (accessed 28 January 2019).

Aristotle (2011) *The Philosophy of Aristotle*, introduction and commentary R Bambrough, trans. A E Wardman. New York: Signet Classics.

Armitage, A, Donovan, G, Flanagan, K and Poma, S (2011) *Developing Professional Practice: 14–19*. Harlow: Pearson.

Armitage, A, Cogger, A, Evershed, J, Hayes, D, Lawes, S and Renwick, A (2016) *Teaching in Post-14 Education and Training,* 5th edition. Maidenhead: McGraw-Hill/Open University Press.

Bandura, A (1977) *Social Learning Theory*. Englewood Cliffs, NJ: Prentice Hall.

Berne, E (1961) *Transactional Analysis in Psychotherapy*. New York: Grove Press.

Berne, E (1964) *Games People Play*. Harmondsworth: Penguin.

Biggs, J (1999) *Teaching for Quality Learning at University*. Maidenhead: SHRE and Open University Press.

Bloom, B S, Engelhart, M D, Furst, E J, Hill, W H and Krathwohl, D R (1956) *Taxonomy of Educational Objectives: The Classification of Educational Goals. Handbook I: Cognitive Domain*. New York: David McKay Company.

Boden, M A (1994) *Piaget*. London: Fontana.

Bruner, J (1960) *The Process of Learning*. Cambridge, MA: President and Fellows of Harvard College.

Canterbury Christ Church University (2018) *Canterbury Christ Church University Apprenticeship Framework*. [online] Available at: www.canterbury.ac.uk/business-and-community/apprenticeships/apprenticeships.aspx (accessed 28 January 2019).

Child, D (1997) *Psychology and the Teacher*, 6th edition. London: Continuum Education.

Clutterbuck, D (nd) *Twelve Habits of the Toxic Mentor*. The Coaching & Mentoring Network Ltd. [online] Available at: www.coachingnetwork.org.uk/information-portal/articles/ViewArticle.asp?artId=41 (accessed 28 January 2019).

Coffield, F, Moseley, D, Hall, E and Ecclestone, K (2004) *Learning Styles and Pedagogy in Post 16 Learning: A Systematic and Critical Review*. London: Learning and Skills Research Centre.

Commission on Adult Vocational Teaching and Learning (2013) *It's about Work... Excellent Adult Vocational Teaching and Learning*. [online] Available at: www.excellencegateway.org.uk/content/eg5937 (accessed 28 January 2019).

Consortium for Research on Emotional Intelligence in Organizations (1998) *Emotional Competence Framework*. [online] Available at: www.eiconsortium.org/pdf/emotional_competence_framework.pdf (accessed 28 January 2019).

DfE (2018) Introduction of T Levels. *Policy Paper*. [online] Available at: www.gov.uk/government/publications/introduction-of-t-levels/introduction-of-t-levels (accessed 28 January 2019).

DfE/BIS (2016a) *Report of the Independent Panel on Technical Education*. London: HMSO. [online] Available at: https://assets.publishing.service.gov.uk/government/uploads/system/uploads/attachment_data/file/536046/Report_of_the_Independent_Panel_on_Technical_Education.pdf (accessed 28 January 2019).

DfE/BIS (2016b) *Post-16 Skills Plan*. London: HMSO.

DfE, ETF and AELP (2017) The Future Apprenticeships course 'End-Point Assessment – Prepare to Deliver', *Presentation 6: Professional dialogues as an assessment instrument*.

DfES (2006) *Leitch Report on Skills: Prosperity for All in the Global Economy – World Class Skills*. London: HMSO.

Education and Skills Funding Agency (2018) *Apprenticeship Funding: Rules and Guidance for Employers May 2017 to July 2018, Version 3*. [online] Available at: https://assets.publishing.service.gov.uk/government/uploads/system/uploads/attachment_data/file/706505/Employer_rules_v3.pdf (accessed 28 January 2019).

Engestrom, Y (1994) *Training for Change*. Geneva: Labour Office.

Entwistle, N (1988) *Styles of Learning and Teaching*. Abingdon: David Fulton.

Gardner, H (2006) *Multiple Intelligences: New Horizons*. New York: Basic Books/Perseus Books Group.

Gatsby Foundation (2018) *Subject Pedagogy for Science, Engineering and Technology Teachers.* [online] Available at: www.gatsby.org.uk/education/programmes/teacher-education-in-FE (accessed 28 January 2019).

Goleman, D (1998) *Working With Emotional Intelligence*. London: Bloomsbury.

Handy, C (1993) *Understanding Organisations*, 4th edition. London: Penguin Random House.

Honey, P and Mumford, A (1982) *Manual of Learning Styles*. London: P Honey.

Houghton, W (2004) *Engineering Subject Centre Guide: Learning and Teaching Theory for Engineering Academics*. Loughborough: HEA Engineering Subject Centre.

Ingle, S and Duckworth, V (2013) *Teaching and Training Vocational Learners*. London: Sage/Learning Matters.

Institute for Apprenticeships (2015) *Junior Journalist*. [online] Available at: www.instituteforapprenticeships.org/apprenticeship-standards/junior-journalist (accessed 28 January 2019).

Institute for Apprenticeships (2017a) *'How To' Guide for Trailblazers*. [online] Available at: https://dera.ioe.ac.uk/28922 (accessed 28 January 2019).

Institute for Apprenticeships (2017b) *Assessment Method Guide*. [online] Available at: www.instituteforapprenticeships.org/developing-new-apprenticeships/assessment-methods (accessed 28 January 2019).

Institute for Apprenticeships (2017c) *Search the Apprenticeship Standards*. [online] Available at: www.instituteforapprenticeships.org/apprenticeship-standards (accessed 28 January 2019).

Institute for Apprenticeships (2017d) *External Quality Assurance*. [online] Available at: www.instituteforapprenticeships.org/quality/external-quality-assurance (accessed 28 January 2019).

Institute for Apprenticeships (2018) *Assessment Method Guide: Workplace Observation*. [online] Available at: www.instituteforapprenticeships.org/developing-new-apprenticeships/assessment-methods/assessment-method-guide-workplace-observation (accessed 28 January 2019).

Klasen, N and Clutterbuck, D (2002) *Implementing Mentoring Schemes: A Practical Guide to Successful Programs*. Oxford: Elsevier.

Knowles, M, Holton, E F and Swanson, R A (2015) *The Adult Learner*, 8th edition. London: Routledge.

Kolb, D A (1984) *Experiential Learning*. Englewood Cliffs, NJ: Prentice Hall.

Kuczera, M and Field, S (2018) *Apprenticeships in England, United Kingdom*. Paris: OECD.

Landsberger, H A (1968) *Hawthorne Revisited: Management and the Worker, its Critics and Developments in Human Relations in Industry*. Geneva, NY: W F Humphrey Press.

Marton, F and Säljö, R (1976) On Qualitative Differences in Learning: Outcome and Process. *British Journal of Educational Psychology*, 46: 4–11.

Maslow, A H (1987) *Motivation and Personality*, 3rd edition. Delhi: Pearson.

Millar, F (2018) T-levels: The Latest in a Series of Quickly Forgotten Vocational Qualifications. *The Guardian*, 12 June.

Mirza-Davies, J (2015) *Apprenticeships Policy, England Prior to 2010*. London: House of Commons Briefing Paper. [online] Available at: https://researchbriefings.parliament.uk/ResearchBriefing/Summary/CBP-7266 (accessed 28 January 2019).

Moodie, G (2002) Identifying Vocational Education and Training. *Journal of Vocational Education and Training*, 54(2).

Office for National Statistics (2018) *Internet Access: Households and Individuals, Great Britain: 2018*. [online] Available at: www.ons.gov.uk/peoplepopulationandcommunity/householdcharacteristics/homeinternetandsocialmediausage/bulletins/internetaccesshouseholdsandindividuals/2018#main-points (accessed 28 January 2019).

Ofqual (2015a) *The Regulated Qualifications Framework*. [online] Available at: https://assets.publishing.service.gov.uk/government/uploads/system/uploads/attachment_data/file/461298/RQF_Bookcase.pdf (accessed 28 January 2019).

Ofqual (2015b) *What Different Qualification Levels Mean: List of Qualification Levels*. [online] Available at: www.gov.uk/what-different-qualification-levels-mean/list-of-qualification-levels (accessed 28 January 2019).

Pemberton, C (2006) *Coaching to Solutions*. Oxford: Elsevier.

Pemberton, C (2013) *Coaching Crib Sheet*.

Pemberton, C and Cray, S (2013) *Confident Conversations: Performance Coaching*. Guildford: Ranmore Consulting.

Polyani, M (1967) *The Tacit Dimension*. New York: Doubleday and Co.

Quinn, F M (2000) *The Principles and Practice of Nurse Education*, 4th edition. Cheltenham: Stanley Thornes.

Ramsden, P (1992) *Learning to Teach in Higher Education*. London: Routledge.

Richard, D (2012) *The Richard Review of Apprenticeships*. London: School for Startups.

Rogers, C (1994) *Freedom to Learn*, 3rd edition. Upper Saddle River, NJ: Prentice Hall.

Schön, D A (1983) *The Reflective Practitioner*. Aldershot: Arena Ashgate Books.

Schön, D A (1991) *The Reflective Turn: Case Studies In and On Educational Practice*. New York: Teachers Press, Columbia University.

Senge, P M (2006) *The Fifth Discipline: The Art and Practice of the Learning Organization*, 2nd edition. London: Random House Business Books.

Shulman, L (1986) Those Who Understand: Knowledge Growth in Teaching. *Educational Researcher*, 15(2): 4–14.

Shulman, L (1987) Knowledge and Teaching: Foundations of the New Reform. *Harvard Educational Review*, 57(1): 1–22.

Shulman, L and Shulman, J (2004) How and What Teachers Learn: A Shifting Perspective. *Journal of Curriculum Studies*, 36(2): 257–71.

Skinner, B F (1938) *The Behaviour of Organisms: An Experimental Analysis*. New York: Appleton-Century-Crofts.

Stevenson, J (1992) Australian Vocational Education: Learning from Past Mistakes? *Vocational Aspects of Education*, 44: 236–7.

Stevenson, J (1998) Finding a Basis for Reconciling Objectives on Vocational Education and Training. *Australia and New Zealand Journal of Vocational Education Research*, 6(2): 134–65.

Strategic Development Network (2016) *The Presentation/Showcase: Under the Bonnet of End-Point Assessment*. [online] Available at: www.strategicdevelopmentnetwork.co.uk/the-showcase-presentation-under-the-bonnet-of-end-point-assessment (accessed 28 January 2019).

Thompson, J (2007) *Plumbing Revision Guide*. Harlow: Harcourt Education Ltd.

Vygotsky, L S (1978) *Mind in Society*. Cambridge, MA: Harvard University Press.

Which? University (2018) *The Complete Guide to Higher and Degree Apprenticeships*. London: HMSO. [online] Available at: https://assets.publishing.service.gov.uk/government/uploads/system/uploads/attachment_data/file/706821/Higher_and_degree_apprenticeships_NAS_Which_Uni_Web__25_.pdf (accessed 28 January 2019).

Whitmore, J (2017) *Coaching for Performance*, 5th edition. Boston, MA: Nicholas Brealey Publishing.

Wikipedia (2018) *Breach of the Peace*. [online] Available at: https://en.wikipedia.org/wiki/Breach_of_the_peace (accessed 28 January 2019).

Wikispaces (2018a) *Mentor Metaphors*. [online] Available at: https://sdttsn.wikispaces.com/file/view/Mentor+Metaphors.pdf (accessed 28 January 2019).

Wikispaces (2018b) *Revised Bloom's Taxonomy: Verbs, Sample Question Stems, Potential Activities and Products*. [online] Available at: eldnces.ncdpi.wikispaces.net/file/view/Blooms_Revised.pdf/517726442/Blooms_Revised.pdf (accessed 28 January 2019).

Wolf, A (2011) *Review of Vocational Education: The Wolf Report*. London: DfE.

# Index